CAXTON
DICTIONARY OF
ENGLISH
GRAMMAR

CAXTON EDITIONS

First published in Great Britain by
CAXTON EDITIONS
an imprint of
the Caxton Publishing Group Ltd
20 Bloomsbury Street
London WC1B 3QA

This edition copyright
© 2000 CAXTON EDITIONS

Compiled and designed
for Caxton Editions by
Superlaunch Limited
PO Box 207
Abingdon
Oxfordshire OX13 6TA

ISBN 1 84067 081 9

A copy of the CIP data for this book is available from
the British Library upon request

Printed and bound in India

CONTENTS

A

a, **an:** the indefinite article. The form *a* is used
before words beginning with a consonant sound
(*a boy*, *a field*, *a game*, *a score*, *a win*). The form
an is used before words beginning with a vowel
sound (*an apple*, *an elephant*, *an inclination*, *an
orifice*, *an upset stomach*). It is the sound of the
initial letter that matters and not the spelling.
Thus *a* is used before a word starting with a *u*
when it is pronounced with a *y* sound, as though it
were a consonant (*a unicorn*, *a useless attempt*).
Similarly, *an* is used before words beginning
with the letter *h* where this is not pronounced
(*an heir*, *an honest man*, *an hour*).

Traditionally *an* was used in pronunciation
before words that begin with an *h* and also begin
with an unstressed syllable, such as *hotel*, but
since it became customary to pronounce the *h*
in such words, we have tended to say as well as
to write *a hotel*. Conversely, today there is an
increasing tendency indiscriminately to use *an*
before any word beginning with an *h*, possibly
stemming from ignorance as to whether the *h*
should be pronounced or not: *an historic victory*,
an horrific accident, *an hysterical woman*.

a~, **an~:** a prefix from Greek, meaning *without*,
not. It is usually prefixed to Greek stems. Older
examples include *agnostic*, *anarchic*, *anonymous*;
modern words have been formed using it, such
as *apolitical*, *asexual*, *atypical*.

abbreviations: words that have been shortened so
as to save space, especially to avoid repetition.
Should the components be separated by full
stops? The tendency now is always to omit them,
whether the initials are written as capital
letters (*MP*, *UFO*, *UK* and *USA*) and separately
pronounced, or written as a pronounceable word

(*faqs*; *see also* **acronyms**). They must not be used if any of the letters are not initials of a full word (*television* has become *TV*, and *worldwide web*, *www*), and should be used fully or not at all; *e.g.* or *ie* are acceptable, but never eg., with a single stop following the two initial letters.

Full stops are rarely used after contractions, (abbreviations to the first and last letters of a word: *Dr*, *Mr*, *Rd*, *St*), and it is a matter of taste whether to use them following abbreviations to the first few letters, as in *Mar.* (*March*), *Prof* (*Professor*). Many people prefer to retain the full stop following the initials of a person's name, even if they are omitted elsewhere in the text.

Plurals are generally formed simply by adding a lower-case *s* (*Drs*, *JPs*, *TVs*).

ablative: a case in Latin grammar expressing *by*, *with* or *from*. This does not exist in English, prepositional phrases being used in its place.

~**able:** a suffix meaning *that can be*, that may be appended to any transitive verb to make an adjective with that sense (*dividable*, *referable*, *tenable*); *see* **adjective**.

abstract noun: one which is the name of a thing that cannot be touched but refers to a quality, concept or idea (*anguish*, *anxiety*, *bravery*, *courage*, *daring*, *dash*, *excitement*, *fear*, *grief*, *hope*, *innocence*, *jeopardy*, *knowledge*, *longing*, *loyalty*, *mirth*, *need*, *optimism*, *pain*, *quality*, *resistance*, *sensibility*, *sensitivity*, *tenderness*, *uneasiness*, *vanity*, *want*, *wisdom*, *xenophobia*, *yearning*, *zeal*); *contrast with* **concrete noun**.

accent: commonly refers to features of inflection and pronunciation that signal regional or social identity (*a Liverpudlian accent*).

It also refers to the symbols used on the

letters of some foreign words to indicate vowel length, vowel quality, or unusual pronunciation. These words have been borrowed and adopted into English, and as they have become more widespread, the accents have been more frequently omitted. An actor's part in a play is now usually spelt *role*, but originally was spelt *rôle*, with the circumflex accent on the *o*.

The accent is most likely to be retained if it affects the pronunciation in English. Thus *fiancé* and *soufflé* usually retain the acute accent on the final *e*, although the cedilla is frequently omitted from beneath the *c* in words such as *façade* (facade), despite being there to show that the *c* is pronounced softly like an *s*, rather than a hard *k*.

- **acute** runs diagonally from top right to bottom left over the top of a vowel, found in English in some words of French origin: *cliché*, *café*.
- **cedilla** is beneath the letter *c*, again in some words of French origin, for example *soupçon*.
- **circumflex** a 'hat' above a vowel, again in some words of French origin, for example *débâcle*, *crêpe*, *dépôt*, *Côte d'Azure*.
- **grave** runs diagonally from top left to bottom right over the top of a vowel. It is more frequently retained in English than the others, in words derived from French (*après*, *discothèque*, *mise en scène*, *son et lumière*).
- **tilde** above the letter *n* in some words of Spanish origin, for example *Señor*, *mañana*, which although widely understood are not fully anglicised.
- **umlaut**, a **diacritic** (¨) indicating a changed vowel sound, especially in Germanic languages (*ä*, *ë*, *ï*, *ö*, *ü*). It is hardly ever used in

English, often being transliterated by using an *e* following the now unaccented letter even in proper names (*Goering* for *Göring*) or undergoing a complete re-spelling (*Cologne* for *Köln*).

The word *accent* is also used to mean emphasis, as in *The accent today is on basic skills*.

accusative: a case in Latin grammar (also called the objective case) which identifies the **object** of the verb. In the phrase *she watched him*, the pronoun *him* would be in the accusative.

acronyms: like some **abbreviations**, are formed from the initial letters of several words. Unlike abbreviations, however, acronyms are pronounced as words rather than as a sequence of letters and so are written without full stops. For example, *NATO* (North Atlantic Treaty Organization) can be pronounced *nato* and is therefore an acronym, unlike *UK* (United Kingdom) which is pronounced as two separate letters.

Most acronyms are written in capital letters. However, when the words do not have capital letters before abbreviation, such as *<u>a</u>cquired <u>i</u>mmune <u>d</u>eficiency <u>s</u>yndrome*, the acronym, *Aids*, is written with an initial capital, the rest of the letters being lower case, as for a **proper noun**, which distinguishes it from the verb *to aid*.

Acronyms which refer to a piece of scientific or technical equipment are written without a capital, for example *laser* (*<u>l</u>ight <u>a</u>mplification by <u>s</u>imulated <u>e</u>mission of <u>r</u>adiation*).

active voice: the forms of a verb which are used when the subject is a person or thing that does something. For example, in *The dog chased the cat*, the sentence, and the verb-form used in it, are active, because the subject *of* the action,

The dog, has performed it. By contrast, in *The cat was chased by the dog*, the subject *to* the action, *The cat*, didn't perform it; this sentence, and the verb-form used, are said to be in the **passive voice**.

acute accent: *see* **accent**.

adjectival clause: a subordinate clause that describes or modifies a noun or pronoun; *see* **relative clause**, the name by which it is better known.

adjective: identifies an attribute of a noun or pronoun, or gives additional information about it. Adjectives tell us about the noun's colour (*green eyes*, *red hair*, *yellow curtains*), its size (*big man*, *massive ballroom*, *minute spare bedroom*, *small baby*), its number (*five carrots*, *one hundred files*, *three notebooks*), its quality (*dejected supporters*, *despondent players*, *unhappy manager*), or its classification (*civil engineering*, , *cutting-edge technology*, *futuristic design*, *Gothic architecture*, *modern materials*, *state-of-the-art computer*).

Several adjectives may modify one noun or pronoun: *a large, red, double-decker, London bus*; *the small, blue, lace-up shoes*. Their order is flexible and can vary according to the emphasis one wishes to place on the various adjectives. One common sequence is size, quality, colour and classification: *a tall, loud, ruddy-faced dairy farmer*. Generally, the most striking feature comes first: *a teeny-weeny, pale blue-green bikini*.

Adjectives in English do not change their form; they remain the same whether the noun to which they refer is singular or plural, or masculine or feminine. Not all adjectives appear before the noun; for their positioning *see* **attributive adjective**, **predicative adjective**.

Many adjectives are formed from either the past participles of verbs, and so end in *~ed* (*beguiled, bored, bruised, intrigued, liked*), or from the present participles and so end in ~*ing* (*accommodating, living, loving, obliging, working*).

Several adjectives ending in ~*ical* are formed by adding ~*al* to nouns ending in ~*ic* (*comical, logical*). Sometimes the adjectives ending in ~*ical* are formed from nouns that end in ~*ics* (*acoustical, ethical, hysterical, statistical, tropical*). Several adjectives ending in ~*ic* are formed from nouns ending in ~*ics* (*acoustic, aerobic, economic, electronic, linguistic*).

Other common adjectival endings include ~*ful* (*awful, doubtful, grateful, helpful, thankful, useful, wonderful*). They also include ~*less* (*baseless, bottomless, boundless, careless, clueless, colourless, helpless, moonless, motionless, thankless*).

The suffix ~*able* may be appended to any transitive verb to make an adjective with the sense *that can* (or *may*, or *must*) *be* ~*ed*; (*accountable, actionable, adorable, answerable, dividable, dutiable, forgivable, preferable*). When the verb ends in mute ~*e*, this is dropped, except after soft *c* or *g* (*drivable, usable*, but *manageable, pronounceable*); but if the verb ends in ~*y* and in addition the letter preceding it is a consonant, this becomes ~*iable* (*justifiable, reliable*, but *buyable, enjoyable, payable*).

If the verb ends with the Latin-derived ending ~*ate* this is dropped (*demonstrable*), unless the verb is **disyllabic** (*creatable*).

The following list is intended to include most of the existing ~*ble* adjectives other than ~*able*. Of course, the list can be extended by adding the prefixes *in*~, *un*~ or *non*~ to form the negative or positive forms of the adjectives. Some of them also have an ~*able* form; they are followed by an asterisk *; the use of the ~*able* form is then recommended.

Adjectives ending in ~**ble** *other than* ~**able**

accessible
adducible
admissible
apprehensible
audible
collapsible*
collectible*
combustible
comestible
compatible
comprehensible
compressible
conductible*
connectible*
contemptible
contractible*
convertible
convincible
corrigible
corruptible
credible
deducible
deductible
defeasible
defensible
depressible
descendible*
destructible
diffusible*
digestible
dirigible
discernible*
discerptible

discussible*
dismissible
dissoluble
distensible *or* distendable
divertible
divisible
edible
educible
eligible
excerptible
exhaustible
exigible
expansible *or* expandable
expressible
extendible, extensible *or* extendable
fallible
feasible
feeble
fencible
flexible
forcible
fusible
gullible*
horrible
immiscible *or* unmixable
impartible
impassible
imprescriptible

impressible
incontrovertible
indefeasible
indefectible
indelible
inducible
intelligible
invincible
irascible
irresistible
legible
negligible
noble
omissible
oppressible
ostensible
perceptible
perfectible*
permissible
persuasible *or*
  persuadable
pervertible
plausible
possible
preventible*
producible
protrusible *or*
  protrudable
reducible
reflexible *or*
  reflectable
refrangible *or*
  refractable
remissible
reprehensible
repressible
resoluble
responsible
reversible*
revertible
risible
seducible
sensible
soluble
submersible
suggestible
susceptible
suspensible *or*
  suspendable
suppressible
tangible
terrible
traducible
transmissible
vendible
visible
voluble

See also **comparative adjectives**, **determiner** *and*
interrogative adjective.

adverb: the main function of an adverb is to add to
  our information about another word.

  With a verb, it gives information about the
action. It could be to say how, when or where it
is done, for example:

There is litter everywhere.
She swims gracefully.
We are eating soon.
Adverbs can also
- intensify the meaning of adjectives:
  He's so tall!
  I'm very thirsty.
- affect the meaning of other adverbs:
  He drives so fast!
  I'll dress very quickly!
- affect the meaning of a prepositional phrase:
  She's completely out of her mind.
- affect the meaning of a whole sentence:
  Surprisingly, he didn't mind at all.

There are several different kinds of adverbs, categorised according to the information they provide about the word they modify. They include adverbs of time, place, manner, degree, frequency, probability, duration, and interrogative adverbs.

adverbs of time tell us when something happened (*afterwards, later, now, soon, yesterday*), as in *He's going to leave afterwards; He'll be getting ready later; He's ready now; I think he'll arrive soon; He was due to arrive yesterday.*

adverbs of place tell us where something happened (*abroad, anywhere, here, hither and thither, outdoors, overhead, somewhere, there, thereabouts, underground*), as in *His family went on holiday abroad; They couldn't find her anywhere; The chained puppy ran hither and thither in distress; We heard a noise outdoors; I haven't ever been there.*

adverbs of manner tell us how something happens and include a wide range of possibilities. Frequently adverbs in this category are formed by adding *~ly* to an adjective. Examples of these include:

adjective	*adverb*
anxious	anxiously
bad	badly
cautious	cautiously
dumb	dumbly
elegant	elegantly
fearless	fearlessly
hot	hotly
interested	interestedly
joking	jokingly
lame	lamely
mean	meanly
narrow	narrowly
pale	palely
quick	quickly
soothing	soothingly
tough	toughly
unwilling	unwillingly
vain	vainly
weak	weakly

There are some adjectives that need modification in some way before the suffix ~*ly* can be adjoined to form the adverbs. For example, with adjectives ending in ~*y*, the *y* changes to *i* before ~*ly* is added. Examples of these include:

adjective	*adverb*
angry	angrily
busy	busily
dry	drily
easy	easily
funny	funnily
happy	happily
merry	merrily
pretty	prettily
silly	sillily
weary	wearily

Note that there are some exceptions such as *shyly*, *slyly*.

Those adjectives ending in ~*e* frequently drop the *e* before adding ~*ly*. Examples of these include:

adjective	*adverb*
feeble	feebly
gentle	gently
true	truly
intelligible	intelligibly

Suffixes other than ~*ly* may be added to adjectives to form adverbs of manner, and these include ~*wards* (*backwards*, *heavenwards*), ~*ways* (*edgeways*, *sideways*) and ~*wise* (*clockwise*).

Some adverbs of manner may take the same form as the adjectives to which they correspond. They include *fast*, *hard*, *solo*, *straight*, *wrong*, as in *The stray dog was caught fast in the bush by its lead*; *He took his father's death hard*; *Don't get me wrong*.

adverbs of degree tell us the strength or intensity of something that happens, and include *adequately*, *almost*, *entirely*, *greatly*, *hugely*, *immensely*, *moderately*, *partially*, *perfectly*, *practically*, *profoundly*, *strongly*, *totally*, *tremendously*, *virtually*, as in: *We are adequately covered by the insurance*; *They enjoyed the theatre immensely*; *The theatre was practically full*; *I strongly disapprove of such shows*; *We were totally unaware of the noise*; *They are tremendously gifted*.

adverbs of frequency are used to tell us the frequency with which something happens, and include *always*, *constantly*, *continually*, *frequently*, *infrequently*, *intermittently*, *never*, *normally*, *occasionally*, *often*, *periodically*, *rarely*, *regularly*, *seldom*, *sometimes*, as in: *I always take breakfast*; *We go to the pub frequently*; *She goes to*

the restaurant occasionally; *I rarely eat meat*; *He
seldom pays the bill*; *We sometimes go on a Tuesday*.

adverbs of probability tell us the chance for
something to happen, and include *certainly*,
conceivably, *definitely*, *doubtless*, *indubitably*,
maybe, *perhaps*, *possibly*, *presumably*, *probably*, as
in: *We will certainly go to the match*; *Our side will
definitely win the cup*; *We will possibly arrive a
little late*; *He will probably wait in the car park
afterwards for us*. Although *hopefully* is an
adverb, it is properly used in the sense *in a
hopeful manner*; *My spaniel gazed at me hopefully
as I took the steaks and sausages off the barbecue*.
In recent years it has often been used at the
beginning of a sentence in order to qualify the
whole sentence, with the meaning that *it is to be
hoped that …*, or even *it is reasonably certain that
…*, as in *Hopefully, the tickets will arrive in time
for us to go to the concert, as they are being sent by
courier*. Although this usage has been widely
adopted in everyday speech, it is still opposed
by purists.

adverbs of duration advise us of the duration (how
long something takes or lasts), and include
always, *briefly*, *eternally*, *forever*, *indefinitely*,
long, *permanently*, *shortly*, *temporarily*, as in: *We
have time to stop briefly for coffee*; *It was a long
walk*; *We expect to arrive shortly*; *We shall stay
temporarily at the hotel*.

adverbs of emphasis add emphasis to the action
described by the verb, and include *absolutely*,
certainly, *just*, *positively*, *quite*, *really*, *simply*, as
in *I absolutely must have that dress*; *I just adore it*;
I quite think it's me; *I'm really not sure now*; *It
simply won't do*.

interrogative adverbs ask or pose questions such

as *how*, *when*, *where*, *why*, as in: *How are you
going to get there?*; *When will you be back?*; *Where
are you going to stay?*; *Why not pack later?*

The interrogative adverb is placed at the
beginning of the sentence, and such sentences
always end with a question mark.

adverbial: means relating to adverbs or elements
that function as adverbs, as in **adverbial
subordinate clause**.

adverbial subordinate clause: a **subordinate clause**
giving information about concession, condition,
manner, place, purpose, reason, result and time.
They usually follow the main clause in the
sentence, but most of them can preceed the
main clause for reason of style or emphasis.

adverbial subordinate clauses of concession are
introduced by conjunctions such as *although,
even though*, *though*, *whereas*, *while*, *whilst*. These
secondary clauses contain a fact that contrasts
in some way with the main clause, as in: *I love
his new car, although I wouldn't have choosen that
colour*; *He does his best at drama school even
though he is not very good actor*; *Whilst I myself do
not like her, I can understand why he does*.

adverbial subordinate clauses of condition are
introduced by conjunctions such as *as long as*, *if,
only if*, *provided*, *providing*, *unless*. These act to
deal with possible situations, as in: *We'll wait
here for as long as it takes to get seen*; *If you don't
keep quiet we will have to leave*; *You can leave only
if the doctor says so*; *Unless the nurse can arrange
for me to have a wheelchair I can't go out*.

Inversion can be used in such clauses instead
of a conjunction, as in *Had you got up on time you
would have seen the start*; *Had I known the whole
family would be coming, I could have baked a*

special cake; *If only interest rates had not gone up, we could have bought a new car this year.*

adverbial subordinate clauses of manner are introduced by conjunctions such as *as, as if, as though, like*, which are used to describe the way that someone behaves or the way in which something is done, as in: *Why does he shout as he does?*; *He looked at her as if he knew her*; *She walked as though she was dancing*; *He entertained us to a wonderful lunch, he cooks just like a professional chef.*

adverbial subordinate clauses of place, introduced by conjunctions such as *everywhere, where, wherever*, indicate the location of an event, the place where, as in: *Everywhere you walked you needed strong shoes*; *He was happy to stay where he was*; *The little boy said he could not remember where he had found it*; *Wherever he went, he was instantly recognised.*

adverbial subordinate clauses of purpose are introduced by conjunctions such as *in order to, so, so as to, so that, to*, and indicate the intention that someone has when doing something, as in: *He did that in order to upset her*; *He added an extra cog so as to make it run smoother*; *They will have to work harder so that it's ready on time*; *They retraced their steps to see if they could find it.*

adverbial subordinate clauses of reason are introduced by conjunctions such as *as, because, since*, and explain why something happens or is done, as in: *He put his Wellington boots on as it was raining*; *We didn't go because we didn't have enough money*; *Since he has broken his arm he has not been able to ride his bike.*

adverbial subordinate clauses of result are introduced by conjunctions such as *so, so that*, and indicate the result of an event or situation, as in: *She did not speak very clearly so the audience had difficulty in understanding her*; *He behaved very well so that he could go out to play*.

adverbial subordinate clauses of time are introduced by conjunctions such as *after, as, as soon as, before, once, since, the minute, the moment, till, until, when, whenever, while, whilst*, and indicate the timing of an event, as in: *He arrived after everyone had gone home*; *She departed as soon as I arrived*; *Once we had said hello, he left*; *I recognised her the moment I saw her, even after all these years*; *We didn't know the total polling count until the following day*; *The thief got away while we waited for the police*.

aero~: a prefix derived from the Greek and meaning *air*, as in *aerodynamics, aeroplane* and *aerospace*; or *aircraft*, as in *aerodrome, aeronaut*.

affective: said of the emotional or attitudinal meaning of an utterance.

affirmative: a sentence or verb that has no marker of negation; *She's dancing, We're going shopping now, We are so happy to be here together again*.

affix: a meaningful form, a letter or a group of letters, that is attached to another form, a **base** or root word to make a more complex word. Affixes can be in the form of prefixes or suffixes. A prefix is an affix that is added to the beginning of a word; thus *un~* in *unkind* is both a prefix and an affix. A suffix is an affix that is added to the end of a word; thus *~ness* in *kindness* is both a suffix and an affix; *see also* **prefix** *and* **suffix**.

agent noun: defines who or what is the doer of (responsible for) the action of a verb. It is normally spelt with an ending of either *~er*, as *driver* and *consumer*, or ~*or*, as *ancestor*, *demonstrator*, but sometimes either of these endings is acceptable, as *adviser / advisor*.

agreement *or* **concord:** a grammatical relationship in which two or more elements in a clause or sentence agree, *i.e.* they take the same number, person or gender. In English the most common form of agreement is that between subject and verb, and this usually involves number agreement. This means that singular nouns are usually accompanied by singular verbs, as in *He drives well*; *He is running late*; *My brother has passed his exams*, and that plural nouns are usually accompanied by plural verbs, as in *They drive well*; *They are running late*; *My brothers have passed their exams*.

However, there are problems, and these arise when the noun in question can be either singular or plural (*audience, choir, class, club, committee, crowd, family, firm, government, group, jury, orchestra, school, staff, the Bank of England, the BBC, the British public*). Such nouns take a singular verb if the user is regarding the people or items referred to by the noun as a group, as in *The family is well remembered in the area, although the youngest son left years ago*. They take a plural verb if the user is regarding the people or items referred to as individuals, as in *The family are contesting his will, although they cannot agree about how best to make a more equitable distribution of the spoils*.

Compound subjects, that is where there are two or more nouns acting as the subject, whether singular or plural, which are joined with *and*, are used with a plural verb (as in *Tracey and I are going to Ibiza on holiday again this year*), unless the two nouns together represent a single concept (as in *gin and tonic*), in which case the verb is in the singular: *Gin and tonic is my husband's favourite drink*.

In the case of alternative subjects (separated by *or*), if the subjects are singular, the verb is also singular; *Mother or child is to die*. Similarly, if the subjects are plural, the verb is also plural, but if the subjects are both singular and plural, as in *Mother or children are to die*; *Is the child or the parents to be blamed?*, there are three possible solutions. One can choose the number of the subject that is nearer to the verb, as shown in both of these examples. This reads reasonably well for the second example, but rather oddly in the first. Another solution is to put one of the subjects at the end of the sentence: *The mother is to die, or the children*; *Is the child to be blamed, or the parents?*. Finally, it is often possible to choose a different verb, that has a single common form for both numbers, such as *must* or *will*: *Mother or children must die*; *Will the child or the parents be blamed?*.

The expressions *a number of* and *a group of* are used with plural nouns and pronouns, and the verb that follows is also plural: *A number of my friends think I should go back there to live*.

The expressions *a lot of* and *the majority of* can be used with either singular or plural nouns and verbs: *A lot of trouble is caused by racism*; *A lot of people have been here today*; *The majority of students were going to attend the demonstration*; *The majority is in favour of the motion*. The preferred form in each case is suggested by whether *a lot* or *the majority* represents *much* or *many*, acting as a group or as individuals: *Much trouble is caused by racism*; *Many people have been here today*; *Many students were going to attend the demonstration*; *Much of the audience is in favour of the motion*.

The words *any*, *none*, *either* and *neither*, when they are used as quantifiers, are followed by *of* + *plural noun* or *pronoun*. The verb is in the singular in a formal style (but often the plural is used in an informal style): *Any of the girls is (are) capable of passing the exam*; *None of them is (are) really motivated*; *Either of the twins is (are) suitable for the job*; *Neither of them is (are) fully qualified*.

When two or more singular nouns acting as the subject are connected with such phrases as *as well as*, *together with* and *plus*, the verb is in the singular: *His elder sister, as well as his brother, is at Trinity College, Dublin*; *The manor-house, together with the gate-house, is up for sale*.

When the subject is a singular noun which is separated from the verb by a number of plural nouns, the verb is in the singular. For example, in *A programme of dates and venues for concerts for the whole season has been published*, the verb is in the singular because *programme* is singular.

Agreement with reference to both number and gender affects pronouns, as in *She hates herself*; *He could have hurt himself*; *They asked themselves why they had done it*. Problems arise when the pronoun is indefinite and so the sex of the person is unspecified. Formerly in such cases the masculine pronouns were assumed to be neutral and so *Each of the applicants was asked to hand in his form* was considered quite acceptable. Feminists disliked this assumption and put forward alternatives, including *Each of the applicants was asked to hand in his or her form*, which is decidedly clumsy. A more euphonious alternative is *Each of the applicants was asked to hand in their form.* Although it is ungrammatical, this convention is becoming quite common in modern usage. To avoid both the clumsiness of the former and the poor grammar of the latter, it is possible to recast the whole sentence in the plural, as in *All the applicants were asked to hand in their forms.*

agro~, agri~: a prefix derived from the Greek and meaning *field*, as in *agrochemicals, agronomy, agricultural, agribusiness.*

~aholic: a suffix formed by analogy with *alcoholic* and meaning *addicted to*, as in *workaholic, shopaholic*. It sometimes takes the spelling *~oholic*, as in *chocoholic*.

allegory: a description in narrative, in verse, prose or drama, which has a hidden or deeper significance as well as the obvious surface meaning of the story. It is used to convey a moral message symbolically, presenting literal characters and events which contain sustained reference to a simultaneous structure of other ideas or events. One such symbolical narration in English literature is John Bunyan's religious allegory *Pilgrim's Progress.*

alliteration: a figure of speech in which a sequence of words begin with the same letter or sound. It is used especially by poets: *red, red rose; In a summer season when soft was the sun; Wherein to swing, sweep, soar*, but in everyday life are better known from 'tongue twisters' such as *Peter Piper picked a peck of pickled peppers.*

allonym: a name an author assumes that belongs to someone else.

alphabet: a writing system in which a set of symbols (letters) represent the phonemes of a language.

also: an adverb, and not a conjunction. However, in speech or in informal writing, it is often used with or instead of *and* or *but*: *and also*, *but also*; or to mean *as well as* (as in *Remember to buy some fruit and vegetables; also some fresh cheese for supper tonight*).

although: a subordinating conjunction that introduces a clause of concession: *I'd like to go out, although it's a bit late*. It can be used in all styles, and can be replaced by *though* or *even though* in informal situations; *see* **subordinate clause**, **adverbial subordinate clause** and **subordinating conjunction**.

alveolar: a description used of a consonant in which the tongue makes contact with the bony prominence behind the upper teeth.

ambi~: a prefix derived from Greek and meaning *two* or *both*, as in *ambidextrous*, *ambivalence*.

ambiguous: a word or sentence which may be understood to have more than one meaning.

amelioration: a change of meaning in which a word loses an original unpleasant sense to an improved one.

an: *see* **a**.

an~: *see* **a~**.

anacoluthon: a sentence which lacks a correct syntactical sequence, so that the first part shows an unexpected break with the second part. Although it could be used as a figure of speech for literary or rhetorical effect, it is more often used accidentally: *We must have our lunch now – whatever possessed you to wear those shoes with that dress, today of all days?*.

anagram: a technical term for shuffling the letters

of a word or a phrase, resulting in a significant combination, as in *the eyes / they see*; *parliament / partial men*; *Piet Mondrian / I paint modern*.

analogy: a logical or grammatical term used to imply a resemblance between two concepts or entities that are being compared, as in *His decisions are rather like the millennium – a long time coming but not really changing the world*.

ananym: a name that has been written backwards.

anapaest *or* **anapest:** a unit of metre that consists of two unstressed (light) beats followed by one stressed (heavy) beat: *un|der|stand*.

anaphora: in grammatical structure a feature that refers back to something that has already been expressed. The last pronoun is anaphoric in *When he saw her, he smiled at her*; *see* **cataphora**.

anastrophe: a figure of speech which refers to an inversion of the usual order of words in a sentence or phrase for emphasis, or rhetorical effect, as in *Me he restored, and him he hanged*, where the object of the verb comes before the subject.

and: called a co-ordinating conjunction because it connects expressions that are grammatically similar. The expressions may be nouns, as in *bread and butter*; verbs, as in *they sang and danced all night*; clauses, as in *John went home and I waited at the station*.

When there are more than two expressions, we usually put *and* before the last one only; *My brother, my sister and I had lunch together*. There is often no comma between the last two items, as in the last example. However, if the last two items are long, we are more likely to use commas; *I spent yesterday playing cricket, drinking beer, and talking about the meaning of life*.

When a co-ordinating conjunction is used, the

subject of the second clause can sometimes be omitted if it is the same as the subject of the first clause, as in *They have been forced to sell the family home and are very sad about it.*

The use of *and* at the beginning of a sentence should be used only for deliberate effect or emphasis, as in *And now for something completely different*, or in informal contexts.

Anglo~: a prefix meaning *English*, as in *Anglo-Saxon, Anglo-French.*

animate: refers to words, especially nouns, that refer to living things, and not to objects or thoughts.

ante~: a prefix derived from Latin, meaning *before*, as in *antecedent, antecessor, antechamber, antedate, antediluvian, antenatal, antenuptial, ante-post*. The opposite of *ante~* is *post~*.

antecedent: the noun or noun phrase in a main clause to which a relative pronoun in a relative clause refers back. Thus in the sentence *The car that bumped into mine was brand new*, the noun *car* is the antecedent. Similarly, in the sentence *I've just spoken to the new neighbour, who is a doctor*, the phrase *the new neighbour* is the antecedent; *see* **relative clause**.

anthimeria: the use of one word class with the function of another in traditional rhetoric, as when *dog*, normally a noun, is used as a verb: '*This evil stalker dogged his victim's footsteps all day and all night*', *said the judge.*

anthropo~: a prefix derived from Greek and meaning *human being*, as in *anthropocentric, anthropogeny, anthropoid, anthropology.*

anthroponomastics: the study of personal names.

anti~: a prefix derived from Greek, meaning *against*. It is used in many words that have been established in the language for a long time, as in *antiphony*, *antipodes* and *antithesis*, but it has also been used to form modern words, as in *antifreeze*, *anti-aircraft*, *anti-malaria tablets*, *antiperspirant*, *anti-tank gun*. The opposite of *anti~* is *pro~*.

anticlimax: a rhetorical term, used when the impressive effect of a climax is cancelled by a final item of inferior importance, as in *The rest of all the acts of Asa, and all his might, and the cities which he built, are they not written in the book of the chronicles of the kings of Judah? Nevertheless in the time of his old age he was diseased in his feet.*

antiphrasis: a figure of speech in which a word or phrase is used in a contrary sense, i.e. opposite to the accepted sense: *Promises are made to be broken*. It is often used to create an ironic or humorous effect: *His mother is ninety years young today*; *There's no such thing as a free lunch*.

antithesis: a figure of speech in which contrasting ideas are balanced for effect: *Make love, not war*; *Marry in haste, repent at leisure*. It is a common figure of speech in literature, as in Alexander Pope's *To err is human, to forgive, divine*.

antonomasia: a figure of speech which involves the use of a personal name or proper name for anyone belonging to a class or group, for example, *his lordship* for *an earl* and conversely *a Napoleon* for *a great conqueror* or *He is such a Machiavelli* for *He is a subtle schemer* (or *politician*).

antonym: a word that is opposite in meaning to another word: thus *day* is an antonym for *night*, *right* is an antonym for *wrong*, and *fast* is an antonym for *slow*. An antonym is the opposite of a **synonym**, and as such may often be found in a thesaurus.

any: a determiner, a quantifier, an adverb or a pronoun.

- As a determiner, it is used with uncountable and plural nouns, in questions and negatives: *Have you got any aspirins?*; *I haven't got any money at all.* It can also be used in positive statements, to refer to the representative of a group, as in *Any actor will tell you that it is easier to perform than to be themselves.*
- As a quantifier, *any* is used with *of + determiner + noun* in questions or negatives: *Do you know any of my friends?*; *I don't still have any of those books that I borrowed from the library last week.* It can also be used in positive statements, to refer to the representative of a group: *It had been the biggest mistake any of them could remember.* For number agreement, *see* **agreement.**
- As an adverb, *any* is used to emphasise a comparative adjective or adverb, or with the adjective *different*, in a question or a negative statement: *Is she any better?*; *If it gets any harder I'm going to stop*; *I don't think you look any different from the way you did last year.*
- As a pronoun, *any* is used to refer to uncountable and plural nouns, in questions and negatives: *I'd like some apples, please. Have you got any?*; *The children needed new school clothes but Kim couldn't afford any.* It is also used in positive sentences, in referring to the representative of a group: *Clean the mussels and discard any that do not close.*

  The equivalent of *any* in affirmative sentences and in some questions is **some.**

anyone: an indefinite pronoun. It should be used only with a singular verb, as in *Has anyone seen* *my keys?*; *Is anyone coming to the shops?*. It should also be followed, where relevant, by a singular, not plural, personal pronoun or possessive adjective: *Has anyone left his or her coat behind?*. This obviously demands more care in casting the sentence in order to make it both grammatical and elegant: *see also* **agreement** or **concord**.

aphasia *or* **dysphasia:** a language disorder which is the result of brain damage. It affects a person's ability to produce or understand grammatical and semantic structure.

aphesis: the loss of an unstressed vowel from the beginning of a word, such as *'mongst (amongst)*, *'neath (beneath)*, *'twixt (betwixt)*.

aphorism: a succinct statement that defines a scientific or general truth in a few words: *More haste, less speed*; see also **proverb**. *Aphorism* should not be confused with *axiom*, a self-evident truth taken for granted as the basis of reasoning; *maxim*, a guiding principle, especially in the practical concerns of life, or *adage*, a long-established saying of universal application.

apocope: the omission of a final syllable, sound, or letter in a word. e.g. the *f* in *Tam O'Shanter*, *light o'my life*; *The huntin', shootin' and fishin' seasons*.

aposiopesis: a figure of speech in which words are omitted or there is a sudden breaking off in the midst of a sentence for dramatic effect, as in *Oh, go to –*, or *If we should fail –*.

apostrophe: a punctuation mark which is used in several different ways:
- to show where letters have been left out of a contracted form: *can't, don't, I'd, I'm*. In dates, when the first two figures of the number of a year are omitted, we can use the apostrophe: *18 September '44*; *The class of '68*.

- Apostrophes are used in genitive (possessive) forms; we add *'s* to a singular noun, *'* to a plural noun ending in ~*s* (*s'*), and *'s* to an irregular plural noun that does not end in ~*s*: *my mother's car*; *the neighbours' garden*; *the children's toys*.

    Singular names ending in ~*s*, ~*x* or ~*z* usually have possessive forms in ~*'s*, especially if they are one-syllable words: *James's son*, *the fox's lair*. However, with many older, foreign and classical names, we just add an apostrophe: *Cervantes' Don Quixote*; *Euripides' play*; *Guy Fawkes' night*.

    Note that apostrophes are often wrongly omitted in modern usage, particularly in the media and by advertisers, as in *mens clubs*, *childrens clothes*, which should be *men's clubs*, *children's clothes*. Equally frequently they are erroneously added, as in *tomato's for sale* and *Beware of the dog's*, which should be *tomatoes for sale* and *Beware of the dogs*. This is partly because of an increasing tendency to minimise punctuation and partly because people are unsure about when to use them.
- Apostrophes are sometimes used with *s* informally to make a plural form for words which are not normally found in the plural: *This project is interesting, but there are too many if's*; similarly with letters and numbers: *She confuses B's and D's*; *He died in his late 50's* (although *50s* is preferable, if only on typographical grounds).

    Apostrophe is also a figure of speech in traditional rhetoric, in which an idea, inanimate object, or absent person is addressed as if present: *O Romeo! Romeo! wherefore art thou, Romeo?* and *O Death, where is thy sting?*.

appellative: a personal name used as an everyday word, such as *sandwich*; *see also* **eponym**.

applied linguistics: the application of theories of linguistics to the solution of practical problems.

apposition: a series of nouns or noun phrases, with the same meaning and grammatical status, which provide further information about another noun or phrase, are said to be in apposition. Both nouns and phrases refer to the same person or thing. In the example *Bertolucci's latest film, a beautiful love story, has just been released*, the expressions *Bertolucci's latest film* and *a beautiful love story* are in apposition. Similarly, in the phrase *His cousin, the chairman of the firm, is on holiday*, the expressions *his cousin* and *the chairman of the firm* are in apposition.

approximant *or* **frictionless continuant:** a consonant in which the lips, palate, tongue and teeth come closer without closing or audible friction.

aptronym: a name that fits a person's occupation or nature, as in *Mr Moneypenny, the banker; Mrs Baker, who has the teashop in the High Street.*

arch~: a prefix derived from Greek and meaning *chief*, as in *archangel, archbishop, archduke*. It may be combined with nouns referring to people, to form new nouns referring to people who are extreme representatives of something; for example, your *arch-rival* is the rival you most want to beat, your *arch-enemy* the one most likely to murder you.

~arch: a suffix derived from Greek and meaning *chief, ruler*, as in *monarch* and *plutarch*.

archaism: an obsolete word or phrase, *i.e.* one that is no longer in general written or spoken use.

areal linguistics: *see* **geographical linguistics**.

argot: a special vocabulary used in public by a

members of a social group in order to disguise the meaning, like the slang originally used by vagabonds. It is now more loosely used, like **jargon**, to mean any sort of special vocabulary.

~arian: a suffix derived from Latin, meaning either *a supporter of*, as in *libertarian*, or *one connected with*, as in *librarian*.

article: *see* **a, definite article, indefinite article, the**.

articulation: the physiological movements used in modifying a flow of air to make speech sounds.

articulator: a vocal organ involved in the production of a speech sound.

articulatory phonetics: that branch of phonetics involved with the study of the way in which speech sounds are produced by the vocal organs.

as: a conjunction which can introduce an **adverbial subordinate clause**, either of *time* (*I saw the bus departing as I arrived at the station*); *manner* (*He behaved as he said he would*), or *reason* (*As it's Sunday he had a lie-in*).

It is also used in the *as … as* construction: *He doesn't play as well as his sister does.* The construction may be followed by a subject pronoun or an object pronoun, according to the sense. In *She plays as well as he*, a slightly shortened form of *She plays as well as he does*, the word *he* is a subject pronoun. In informal English the subject pronoun often becomes an object pronoun, as in *She plays as well as him*, even though the meaning of the two sentences is identical. In the sentence *They hate their father as much as her*, the pronoun *her* is an object and the sentence means *They hate their father as much as they hate her*, but in the sentence *They hate their father as much as she*, the pronoun *she* is a subject and the sentence means *They hate their father as much as she does*; *see* **subordinate clause**, **adverbial subordinate clause** and **subordinating conjunction**.

ascender: the part of a letter that projects above the height of the lower-case *x* (the *x-height*).

aspect: the length or kind of temporal activity denoted by a verb, i.e. the completion or non-completion of an action.

aspiration: the audible breath that can accompany the articulation of a sound, as in *pen* (p̲h̲en).

assimilation: the influence that one sound can exert upon a neighbouring sound, so that the two sounds become more alike.

associative meaning: the association of sense, i.e. associations that are not part of the word's basic meaning: *cow = milk, cheese*.

assonance: a form of vowel rhyme, as in *baby* with *chary, feel* with *need, mate* with *shape*.

asterisked form *or* **starred form:** in a dictionary or reference book indicates either an unacceptable usage, or a word for which the root is inferred to have existed but is not recorded.

astro~: a prefix derived from Greek, meaning *star*, as in *astrodome, astrolabe, astrologer, astrology, astronaut, astronomy*.

asyndeton: a figure of speech from which the conjunctions have been omitted, in order to achieve an economic form of expression for dramatic or literary effect: *I came, I saw, I conquered*.

~athon: a suffix meaning *large scale* or *long-lasting*, relating to a contest or event, e.g. *swimathon*. These words are formed by analogy with the Greek-derived word *marathon*, and thus *swimathon* means swimming marathon. They often refer to events undertaken for charity.

attested: in reference to linguistic forms where

there is evidence of present or past usage.

attributive adjective: an adjective or other form that is placed immediately before the noun and that modifies the noun within the noun phrase: *a black dress*; *the big table*; *a delicious meal*. Here, *black*, *big* and *delicious* are attributive adjectives.

audio~: a prefix derived from Latin, meaning *I hear*. It is found in several words that have been established in the language for a long time, as in *audible*, *audition*, *auditory*, but it is also used to form many more recent words pertaining to sound, especially broadcast sound: *audio-typist*, *audio-cassette* and *audio-visual*.

auditory phonetics: a branch of phonetics that studies the way people perceive sound.

auto~: a prefix derived from Greek, meaning *of* or *by itself*: *autobiography*, *autocephalous*, *autocrat*, *automatic*, *automobile*, *autopilot*.

auxiliary language: the adopted language used by different speech communities for purposes of communication.

auxiliary verb *or* **helping verb:** one which is used in forming the tenses, moods and voices of other verbs. The basic ones which can be used as auxiliary verbs or as normal verbs are *to be*, *to do* and *to have*. **Modal verbs** such as *can* and *will* are also sometimes called auxiliaries.

The verb *to be*, when used as an auxiliary verb with the present participle or *~ing* form of the main verb, forms the continuous present tense: *They are living abroad just now*; *We were thinking of going on holiday but we changed our minds*.

The verb *to be* can also be used as an auxiliary verb with the past participle of the main verb to form the passive voice: *English is spoken here*; *These toys are manufactured in China*.

The verb *to do* is used as an auxiliary verb along with the main verb to form negative sentences: *He does not believe her*. It is also used along with the main verb to form questions: *Does he know that she's gone?*, and to form sentences in which the verb is emphasised: *She does want to go*.

The verb *to have* is used as an auxiliary verb along with the past participle of the main verb to form the perfect tenses: *They have filled the post*; *She had realised her mistake*; *They wished that they had gone earlier*.

baby talk: a simplified style of speech used by adults to very small children.

back: a sound that is made either in the back part of the mouth or with the back part of the tongue.

back formation: the process of word formation in which a new word is formed by removing an element from an existing word. This is a reversal of the usual process, since many words are formed by adding an element to a base or root word. Examples of back formation include *to burgle* from *burglary*; *to donate* from *donation*; *to eavesdrop* from *eavesdropper*; *to edit* from *editor*; *to enthuse* from *enthusiasm*; *to intuit* from *intuition*; *to liaise* from *liaison*; *to reminisce* from *reminiscence*; *to televise* from *television*.

back slang: a form of secretive language in which words are written backwards.

base or **root:** refers to the basic uninflected form of a verb, and is found in the infinitive form (*to go, to take*), and in the imperative form (*Go away! Take it!*). It is also the form taken by the verb in the present indicative tense – with the exception of the third person singular – (*I always go there*

after work; *They go there regularly after work*).
Base also refers to the irreducible, minimal form
of a word to which affixes can be added, and in
this sense it is known as the *root* or *stem*. For
example, *crisp* is the base in *crispness*; *feature* is
the base in *featureless*, and *histor* is the base in
historical.

bathos: an extreme, frequently ludicrous, form of
anticlimax; from the sublime to the ridiculous:
She stormed out in a fury and her new shoes.

be: *see* **auxiliary verb**.

because: a conjunction that introduces an
adverbial subordinate clause of reason: *They sold
the pram because the baby has outgrown it*; *She
never has time to see me because she is so busy*).
However, it is often used incorrectly: *The reason
they went home is because they were tired* should
be rephrased as either *The reason that they went
home is that they were tired* or *They went home
because they were tired*.

before: may be either a preposition, an adverb or a
conjunction. As a preposition it means either
coming or *going in front of* in time: *It was the bus
before this one*, or in place: *She stood before him in
the dark*. As an adverb it means *at a time
previously*: *I've seen you before*; *He has been here
before*. As a conjunction it introduces an
adverbial subordinate clause of time: *The taxi
arrived before she was ready to go*.

bi~: a prefix derived from Latin, meaning *two*,
that forms words in English in which it means
two (*bicycle*, *bifold*, *bilateral*, *bilingual*, *biped*) and
other words in which it means *twice*. It can also
mean *half* (*bi-weekly* and *bi-monthly*, which can
mean either twice per week / month or once in
every two weeks / months).

biblio~: a prefix derived from Greek, meaning *book*, as in *bibliomania*, *bibliography*, *bibliophobia*.

bidialectal: someone who can speak in two dialects.

bilabial: a consonant that is formed by using both lips.

bilingual: someone who speaks two languages with equal fluency.

bio~: a prefix derived from Greek, meaning *life* or *living material*: *biochemistry*, *biodegradable*, *biography*, *biologist*, *bionics*, *bioscope*, *biotic*.

bisyllable: a word with two syllables.

blend: a word formed by the merging of two other words or elements (*breakfast* + *lunch* = *brunch*; *camera* + *recorder* = *camcorder*; *chocolate* + *~oholic* = *chocoholic*; *motor* + *hotel* = *motel*).

body language: a communication that is expressed by body movements, positions and appearances, including facial expressions, hand gestures and the bodily positioning of the speakers; known in more academic circles as *phatic communication*.

bold *or* **bold face:** a typeface that is thicker than normal type weight and so appears blacker. It is used for emphasis or to highlight certain words, for example the **headwords** or **entry words** in this book, which have been so set.

book titles: may cause problems in punctuation. They should appear exactly as they do on the title of the original book, but when this is not known, or if the title has been printed in capital letters throughout, the first letter of the first word, and of the following main words of the title are in capital letters, and those of words of lesser importance, such as the articles, prepositions and co-ordinate conjunctions, are in lower-case letters, as in *The Hitchhiker's Guide to the Galaxy*. The manner in which they are treated in publications depends largely on the house style of the publisher. Generally in books, and in some newspapers, titles of publications quoted are given in italic: *Oxford Companion to the English Language*. Others prefer to put book titles in quotation marks, as in 'The Rudiments of English Grammar', and this is the only effective option in handwritten text. Such a convention can make use of either single or double quotation marks: thus either 'The Elementary Spelling Book' or ''The Elementary Spelling Book'' is possible, provided that the writer is consistent throughout any one piece of writing. Any punctuation within the title itself should be used exactly as in the original, as in *Love's Labour's Lost*; *Philaster, or Love Lies Bleeding* and *Venice Preserv'd, or A Plot Discovered*. Note that the use of capital letters in the last of these three titles is as in the original.

Academic and scientific journals in particular often have very precise rules about the way in which they present such titles, in order to differentiate obviously and easily between the names of individual papers or poems included within a journal or anthology, the name of the publication as a whole, and its volume and / or serial number and date of publication. These sets of rules vary enormously, but for general purposes consistent use of either single or double quotation marks, and the exact form of the original title, is adequate for the titles of books, films, and the names of ships, all of which should be clearly distinguished from the surrounding text.

borrowing: refers to the taking over of a word,

idiom or phrase from one language or dialect
into another. These borrowings may be thus
referred to, or described as loan words. Many
words borrowed into English have been totally
assimilated as to spelling and pronunciation.
Others have remained obviously different and
retain their own spelling and / or pronunciation,
as in *raison d'être*, borrowed from the French.
These are frequently set in *italic type* in
publications. Many of them have been part of
the English language since the Norman Conquest,
so that they are no longer thought of as being
foreign words.

French, Latin and Greek have been the main
sources of our borrowings over the centuries.
However, we have borrowed extensively from
other languages as well. These include Arabic,
from which we have borrowed *algebra*, *alkali*,
almanac(k), *assassin*, *cypher*, *hazard*, *safari*,
scarlet and *talisman*, and from the Aboriginal
language of Australia have come *boomerang* and
kangaroo. The Celtic languages have yielded
bog, *brogue*, *clan*, *slogan* and *whisky*.

Sampan has been borrowed from Chinese;
bonsai, *judo* and *tycoon* have been adopted from
the Japanese and *rattan* from Malay.

From German we have borrowed *frankfurter*,
kindergarten, *schnitzel*, *schnorkel* and *waltz*, as
well as some words dating from the Second
World War, such as *blitz* and *flak*; more recently
we have added ~*fest* as in *beerfest*, and ~*meister*.

From Hebrew we have *alphabet*, *camel*,
cinnamon and *maudlin*, as well as more
contemporary words of Yiddish like *bagel*,
chutzpah, *schmaltz*, *schmuck* and *schtumm*.

The Indian languages have provided us with

many words, originally from the days of the British Empire. They include *dinghy*, *dungarees*, *gymkhana*, *jungle*, *pundit* and *shampoo*, and like the European languages, they now provide a rich array of culinary words such as *chutney*, *bhajee*, *poppadom*, *samosa* and *vindaloo*.

Italian has given us many terms relating to architecture and the arts. These include *corridor*, *fresco*, *loggia*, *mezzanine*, *niche*, *parapet*, *pastiche*, *piano*, *opera*, *soprano* and *tempo* as well as such food terms as *cappucino*, *espresso*, *pasta*, *pizza*, *risotto*, and *ciabiatta*. It also gave us *influenza*.

We have borrowed from the Netherlands words relating our common interest in the sea, such as *deck*, *cruise*, *sloop* and *yacht*. Through its Afrikaans connection we have borrowed *apartheid* and *trek*. From Norse and the Scandinavian languages have come a wide variety of common words including some modern sporting terms such as *ski* and *slalom*.

From the native North American languages have come *anorak*, *kayak*, *raccoon*, and *toboggan*, while from the South American languages have come *chocolate*, *chilli*, *potato*, and *tobacco*.

Language is continually developing and expanding and thus the borrowing process will continue as new technology, new uses, and new relationships broaden our understanding and adaptability.

both: can be used as a determiner (*He broke both his arms*; *He lost both his sons in the war*); a pronoun (*I don't mind which house we rent. I like them both*; *Neither of them work here. The boss sacked them both*); a conjunction (as in *He both likes and admires her*; *She is both talented and honest*). *Both* can sometimes be followed by *of*, in which case it is a quantifier. *Both their children are grown up* and *Both of their children are grown up* are equally acceptable. However, care should be taken to avoid using *both* unnecessarily: in the sentence *The two items are both identical*, it is redundant.

~**bound:** a suffix meaning *physically confined* (as in *housebound*) or *mentally confined* (as in *spellbound*), but it can also mean *obligated* (as in *duty-bound*).

bracketing: a means of showing the internal structure of a string of elements, as in *(The gang)(built)(a road)*.

brackets: a pair of correlative punctuation marks that are used to enclose information that is in some way additional to the main statement. The information so enclosed is called *parenthesis* and the pair of brackets enclosing it are known typographically as *parentheses*. The bracketted information is entirely additional and could be removed without affecting either the thrust or the structure of the statement. Brackets interrupt the flow of the main statement in the same way as commas and dashes, but indicate a more clear-cut interruption.

Material contained within brackets can be:
- one word: *They had a lovely holiday in Gien (France)*; *On holiday we ate lots of calamari (octopus)*.
- dates: *The first novel by Evelyn Waugh (1902–66) was* Decline and Fall, *published in 1928*; *The first World War (1914–18) was a horrific event*.
- a phrase: *We drank kir (a delicious cocktail) all evening*; *Crème de cassis (blackcurrant liqueur) is the basis of the cocktail kir*.

- a clause: *We ate a meal (such as it was) in the shelter of the barn*; *They ate out at the* Inebriated Newt *(as it was called) before returning home.*
- a complete sentence: *He was determined (we don't know why) to tackle the problem alone*; *She made it clear (nothing could be more clear) that she was not interested in the offer.* Sentences that appear in brackets in the middle of a sentence are not usually given an initial capital letter or a full stop.

When the expression within brackets comes at the end of a sentence, the full stop should follow the second bracket. When there is a complete sentence within the brackets, which comes between two other sentences, it is treated like a normal sentence with an initial capital letter and a closing full stop before the closing bracket: *She never seems to do any homework. (She is always either out with her friends or out with her pony.) Despite this, she always seems to fare well in the examinations.*

Punctuation of the main statement is unaffected by the presence of the brackets and their enclosed material except that any punctuation that would have followed the word before the first bracket follows the second bracket, as in *He goes to a school (I am not sure exactly where), that is a long bus ride from here.*

There are various shapes of brackets. Round brackets are the most common type. Square brackets are sometimes used to enclose information that is contained inside other information already in brackets, or in a piece of writing where round brackets have already been used for some other specific purpose. Thus in a dictionary if round brackets are used to

separate off the pronunciation, square brackets
are sometimes used to separate off the
etymologies: *Etymon* (et'i-mon), *n. the true
origin of a word; an original root; the genuine or
literal sense of a word* (rare). *[Neut. of Gr.* etymos,
true.]

Square brackets are also used for editorial
notes in academic or scholarly work where the
material contained within the brackets would
otherwise interupt the flow of the main
statement more than is normally the case with
bracketed material. Angle brackets and brace
brackets tend to be used in more technical
contexts, for example in multi-line maths.

broad: describes speech which, when transcribed,
shows only the major phonetic contrasts. It
may be difficult to understand until the ear
becomes accustomed to it.

buildings: the proper name of a building, if it has
one, should have an initial capital; as should
the common noun that may be part of this
name: *the Taj Mahal*, *Sydney Opera House*, *the
Leaning Tower of Pisa* and *the Empire State
Building*. Occasionally the building may have
the same name as the organisation that
occupies it, in which case it may be preceded by
a definite article which takes a capital letter, as
in *The National Portrait Gallery*; *see below*.

businesses and organisations: generally in their
names or titles, the initial letters of the main
words of the title should be in capital letters
and the words of lesser importance, such as the
articles, co-ordinating conjunctions and
prepositions, should be in lower case throughout
(*Mayflower Chinese Takeaway*; *Aerobics for All*),
unless they form the first word of the title, as in

The Aluminium Window Company Limited.
Obviously, when the names of people are
involved these should have initial capital
letters, as in *Black, Brown & Hobbs Associates*.

but: a conjunction that connects two opposing
ideas, and also a co-ordinating conjunction, in
that it connects two elements of equal status.
These elements may be words (*not in but out*),
phrases (*shouting aloud but not being heard*) or
clauses (*The train is due to depart but the driver
has not arrived yet*). *But* should not be used when
no element of contrast is present. Thus the
following sentence should be rephrased, at least
in formal English *He is not a professional
footballer but an amateur player*. The two clauses
are agreeing, not disagreeing, with each other
and so strictly speaking *but* should not be used.
The use of *but* at the beginning of a sentence
should be used only for deliberate effect of style
or emphasis, or in informal contexts, as it is
grammatically incorrect to use a conjunction
at the beginning of a sentence.

by~: a prefix meaning anything of minor
importance, a subsidiary (as in *by-product*, *by-
road*). It can also mean *around*, as in *bypass*.

byname: a supplementary name that is added to
someone's personal name, intended as an aid to
identification. It sometimes replaces the
original name entirely: *Ethelred the Unready*.

caesura: a break in the rhythm of a line of poetry.
calligraphy: the art of beautiful handwriting.
capital letter: is used as the initial letter of a
proper noun, including the names of continents,
countries, cities, rivers and mountains: *Asia*,
India, *Bombay*, *the River Nile*, *Mount Everest*. The

names of people, both their first names and their surnames, have initial capital letters: *Brigitte Bardot, Arthur Miller*. Initial capital letters are also used in English for the days of the week, the months of the year and the names of public and religious holidays: *Monday, Tuesday, Wednesday, January, February, March, Good Friday, Christmas Day*. Initial capital letters are used for the books of the Bible, and points of the compass are spelt with an initial capital letter if they are part of a specific geographical feature or region, as in *South Pole*. In general, however, initial capitals are not otherwise used for points of the compass or for their related derivatives: *to the east, northern, southernmost, westerly*.

Initial capital letters are usually used in the titles of books. Only the main words are capitalised (*Animal Farm, Anne of Green Gables*); prepositions, determiners and the articles are left in lower-case, unless they form the first word of the title; *see* **book titles**.

Initial capital letters are necessary in trade names (*Dettol, Harpic, Hoover, Persil*); however it should be noted that verbs formed informally from trade names are not spelt with an initial capital letter: *She hoovered the carpet*, although in advertising, where the purpose is to keep the product name in the public eye, this is not so: *He Fed-Exed it to his friend in Washington, DC*.

For capital letters in direct speech *see* **direct speech**; for capital letters in abbreviation and acronyms *see* **abbreviations** and **acronyms**.

cardi~: a prefix derived from Greek and meaning *heart*: *cardiac, cardiogram, cardioid, cardiology*.

cardinal number: the basic form of a numeral,

numbers such as *one*, *two*, *three*, as distinct from **ordinal numbers** which refer to numbers in the form *first*, *second*, *third*.

cardinal vowels: a set of reference points, that are based on auditory and articulatory criteria, is used to identify vowels.

caret: a diacritic (ʌ) used to indicate that a missing letter, word or more extensive matter needs to be inserted into a line of text.

caretaker speech *or* **motherese:** that used by adults when talking to children.

case: the form of a noun, adjective or pronoun showing its grammatical relationship to other words in an inflecting language.

catalect: part of a corpus of literary work seen as separate from the rest of an author's output.

cataphora: a feature in grammar that refers forward to another unit. The pronoun is cataphoric in *Peter said this*; *see also* **anaphora**.

cavity: a chamber in the vocal tract that is anatomically defined.

cedilla: *see* **accent**.

centre: in phonetics refers to the top part of the tongue that is involved in the forming of central sounds.

centring diphthong: a diphthong second element of which involves a movement towards the centre of the vowel area.

channel: the selected medium for communication, for example oral or written.

character: an individual graphic sign deployed in a writing system, including one that is not part of an alphabet; *see also* **logogram**, **logograph**, **timbre**.

chiasmus: a term derived from Greek, meaning *cross-fashion*. A balanced pattern of parallel expressions, in which the sequence of elements is used in the reverse order in the second: *do not live to eat, but eat to live; necessity is the mother of invention, but mothers are the invention of necessity*.

chirography: the study of the forms and styles of handwriting.

chronogram: a phrase or sentence in which letters which are also Roman numerals (C, I, L, M, V, X) combine to form a date.

circumflex: *see* **accent**.

circumlocution: a roundabout way, using more words than is necessary, to express oneself.

clause: a group of words, smaller than a sentence but larger than a phrase, containing a finite verb which forms part of a compound or complex sentence; *see* **main clause**, **subordinate clause** *and* **relative clause**.

cleft sentence: one in which a single clause is split into two sections, each with its own verb: *It was Peter who whistled*.

clerihew: a four-line light verse in which the first two lines rhyme with each other and the last two rhyme with each other. It was popularised by Edward Clerihew Bentley (1875–1956). Usually it deals with a person named in the first line, who is then described in a humorous way.

cliché: a hackneyed stereotyped expression which has become so over-used that it no longer conveys much meaning: *a fate worse than death*; *to make the supreme sacrifice*; *it stands to reason* .

click: a sound that is produced by using the velaric air-stream mechanism, used to convey the sound of disapproval. It is usually written *tsk* or *tut*.

clipping *or* **reduction:** the formation of a new word by cutting an existing longer word: *demo / demonstration*; *phone / telephone*; *flu / influenza*).

closed: used in phonology to describe a syllable

ending in a consonant, and in grammar used to describe a word class of limited membership, e.g. pronouns.

closing diphthong: a diphthong, the second element of which entails a movement towards a high vowel position.

closure: a contact made between vocal organs that enables the production of a speech sound.

cluster: a situation at either the beginning or end of a syllable that involves a series of adjacent consonants.

coalescence: the fusing of originally distinct linguistic units, whereby a sound is influenced by a sound that follows, or preceeds, it, as in *good night* fusing to be pronounced *g'night*.

code: a language, or variety of language, that can include a system of signals devised for the sending of messages, especially secret messages.

code switching: said of a speaker who uses more than one language, dialect or variety during a conversation.

codification: the provision of a systematic account of the grammar and vocabulary of a language.

cohesion: the formal linkage between elements of a discourse of text.

collective noun *or* **group noun:** refers to a group of things, animals or people: *army, government*. It is used when the whole group is being considered, as in *flock of sheep, herd of elephants, kindle of kittens, litter of cubs, murmuration of larks, pack of wolves, pride of lions, rookery of penguins, string of racehorses, troop of monkeys, wisp of snipe*).

colloquial: language such as that used in informal conversation.

colon: a punctuation mark (:) the typical function of which within a sentence is to explain, interpret, clarify, amplify and expand upon what has gone before it: *The weather conditions were very bad: almost arctic temperatures*. A capital letter is not usually used after the colon in this context.

The colon may be used to introduce a quotation: *He always uses the quotation: 'Dr Livingstone, I presume?'*, or a list of items, as in *The ingredients for the recipe are: butter, plain flour, milk, mustard, cheese, salt and pepper*.

It is sometimes used between numerals (as in *7:15 a.m.*), in a statement of proportion (*10:1*) and in biblical references (*Exodus:32*). It is used in the titles of some books, for example where there is a subtitle: *The Golden Oldies: pop records of the 1960s*. In less formal writing, the dash (–) may be used instead of the colon.

comma: a very common punctuation mark (,). In modern usage there is a growing tendency towards a system of minimal punctuation and the comma is one of the major casualties of this attitude. There are certain situations in which the comma is still often used, however. One of these is in lists. The individual items in a series of three or more are separated by commas. There is often no comma before the 'and' which precedes the last item: *yellow, pink and purple flowers*. However, when the last two expressions are long, a comma clarifies the sentence: *He was a handsome man, with a wide-open blue eye that seemed sometimes to be looking at nothing, straight black hair brushed rather low on his broad brow, and a well-proportioned frame*. If one of the last two items in a list contains *and* in its own right (as in *At the fish shop you can buy roast chicken, meat pies, fish and chips and sausages*), it is better to put a comma before the *and* which separates the two expressions: *At the fish shop you can buy roast chicken, meat pies, fish and chips, and sausages.*

When there are several adjectives before a noun, the use of commas was formerly standard practice but is now optional: thus both *She wore a short, black, miniskirt* and *She wore a short black miniskirt* are used.

The comma is also used to separate clauses or phrases that are parenthetical or naturally cut off from the rest of a sentence: *My mother, who never arrives late, was up at the crack of dawn.* Commas are used to separate main clauses from non-defining relative clauses: *Rhiannon Davies, who called yesterday, was my friend's sister.* It is essential to use both commas when doing this. In both sentences the clause within the commas can be removed without altering the basic meaning.

Commas are not used to separate main clauses from defining relative clauses: *Was that the woman who called yesterday?*; nor are they usually used to separate main clauses from brief subordinate clauses, unless the subordinate clause precedes the main clause. It is then sometimes followed by a comma, especially if it is a reasonably long clause: *Although it was raining at the time, we had a difficult decision to make.* If the clause is quite short, or if it is a short phrase, a comma is not usually inserted: *Although it rained we left home on time.* The use of commas to separate adverbs like *however* and *nevertheless* from the rest of the sentence to which they are related is now optional. Thus one can write *Nevertheless, you can go* or

Nevertheless you can go. The longer the expression is, the more likely it is to have a comma after it, as in *On the other hand, I may decide to keep you here*.

Commas are necessary to separate terms of address, interjections or question tags from the rest of the sentence (*Please follow me, Madam Speaker, and make yourself comfortable*; *Now, ladies, what may I get you?*; *A nice cup of tea, with sugar?*). They may be used to separate main clauses joined by a co-ordinating conjunction, but this is not usual if the clauses have the same subject or object: *She drew the curtains and turned down the bed cover*. In cases where the subjects are different and the clauses are fairly long, it is best to insert a comma: *They all went out to play, and she was left to do the housework*.

A comma may be inserted to avoid repeating a verb in the second of two clauses, as in *She plays the violin and the piano, her brother the flute*.

command *or* **directive:** an utterence expressed in the imperative mood, intended to get other people to do something: *Sit down!*; *Be quiet!*; *Stop crying!*.

comment clause: a clause that adds a parenthetic remark to another clause: *The reason is, you see, twofold*.

common core: the extent of linguistic features which are used and understood by all speakers.

common noun: a noun such as *building, carpet, chair, dog, lake, mother, person, tree,* or *water* that is not the name of one particular person or thing; *compare with* **proper noun**.

communication: the sending of information by a transmitter and the accurate receiving of this information by a receiver.

comparative adjectives: formed in two different ways; one way is to add *er* at the end of the adjective (*cheaper*), and the other way is to put the adverb *more* before the adjective (*more curious*). The rules and exceptions are as follows:

- adjectives of one syllable form comparatives with ~*er* (*tall* becomes *taller*), and adjectives ending in ~*e* add ~*r* (*late* becomes *later*). Adjectives with one vowel followed by one consonant double the final consonant: *fat* becomes *fatter*.

  There are irregular comparatives; *bad*, *far* and *good* become *worse*, *farther / further*, and *better*. Also, *old* becomes *older* (regular comparative) or *elder* (irregular comparative). The determiners *little* and *much / many* become *less* and *more*.

- adjectives of two syllables ending in ~*y* form their comparatives with ~*ier* (*happy* becomes *happier*). With most two-syllable adjectives, we use *more* (*tiring* becomes *more tiring*). With a few two-syllable articles, both kinds of comparative are possible, although the use of *more* is most common. These adjectives are *common*, *cruel*, *handsome*, *pleasant*, *polite*, *quiet*, *stupid*, *tired*, *wicked*, and words ending in ~*er*, ~*le* and ~*ow*. Examples are:

  common – commoner / more common
  gentle – gentler / more gentle
  hollow – hollower / more hollow

- adjectives that have three or more syllables form their comparatives with *more*: *catastrophic* becomes *more catastrophic*. Words that are derivated from one or two-syllable words, such as *unhappy*, that comes from *happy*, are an exception, and comparatives such as *unhappier* have been established instead.

Some adjectives by their very definitions do not normally have a comparative form, for example *unique*; *see also* **adjective**.

comparative adverbs: normally made with *more*, as in *Could you talk a bit more quietly?*. However, a few adverbs have a comparative form in *~er*. The most important ones are *early*, *fast*, *hard*, *late*, *long*, *near*, *often*, *soon*, and in informal English, *loud*, *quick* and *slow* (these three adverbs are mainly adjectival; they are used as adverbs in informal English).

There are also a few irregularly formed comparatives: the adverbs *badly*, *little* and *much* become *worse*, *less* and *more* respectively; *see also* **adverb**.

comparative linguistics *or* **comparative philology:** the study of the relationship between languages, especially those believed to have a common historical origin; *see also* **historical linguistics**.

complement: the equivalent of the **object** in a clause with a linking or copula verb. In the sentence *John is a butcher*, the expression *a butcher* is the complement. In the sentence *John is a good butcher*, the expression *a good butcher* is the complement. In the sentence *His son seems an excellent beef butcher*, the expression *an excellent beef butcher* is the complement.

complex preposition: a type of preposition consisting of more than one word, and more particularly, to one where a noun or noun phrase is both preceded by and followed by single prepositions, for example *on account of*; *compare with* **prepositional phrase**, **preposition**.

complex sentence: a type of sentence in which there is a main clause and a subordinate clause or clauses. The sentence *We went to Blackpool although we were not keen* is a complex sentence, since it is composed of one main clause and one subordinate clause (*although we were not keen*). The sentence *We wondered why we had gone and what we would see* is a complex sentence since it has a main clause and two subordinate clauses ('*why we had gone*' and '*what we would see*'); *compare with* **compound sentence** *below*.

compound sentence: a type of sentence which has multiple main clauses linked by a co-ordinating conjunction such as *and*, *or* or *but*: *We played for the Cup and we won handsomely*). They may be easily recognised because each clause may, in principle, stand as a sentence on its own.

There are other compound sentences in which one of the elements has been omitted by **ellipsis**, as in *I bought the red dress and Jenny the blue*, where the verb *bought* has been omitted in the second clause; *compare with* **complex sentence**.

computer language: a system of symbols specially devised for programming and interacting with computers, which has its own logic.

concord: *see* **number agreement**.

concordance: an alphabetical list of the important words used in a particular text, usually with citations of the passages concerned.

concrete noun: describes something which one can touch, a physical entity (*book*, *carpet*, *carrot*, *chair*, *clothes*, *pea*, *pen*, *potato*, *shoes* and *table*), as opposed to **abstract nouns**, which lack this dimension (*dream*, *idea*, *thought*).

conditional: a tense made of the auxiliary *would* followed by the bare infinitive of the verb. The first person may be either *would* or *should*. Both of these forms can be contracted (as in *I'd go*;

she'd fly). The main uses of the conditional are:

- in sentences with *if*, often with another verb in the subjunctive: *He'd leave her if she wasn't so rich*. This use gave its name to the **conditional clause**.
- instead of *shall* or *will* in reported speech, after a verb in the past: *'I have to go' I explained* becomes *I explained I'd have to go*.
- to express the idea of 'future in the past': *When I looked at the list of books I had to read, I almost fainted*; *It wouldn't be easy to read them all before the exams*; *I should have to work much harder than I'd done in previous years*.
- with verbs such as *like* and *prefer*, to make polite requests and offers: *What would you like? – I'd like a glass of wine, please*.

It is important to note that *would* and *should* are not always used to express the conditional. For example, *would* is used to express past habits (*As a child, I used to be scared of the dark and I would always run to the light switch at the end of the corridor*). *Should* is often used to express advice, comment or a recommendation: *Sometimes the assistant is not as helpful as he should be*.

conjunction: a word used to connect clauses or sentences, or words in the same clause. There are two types. A co-ordinating conjunction is a word such as *and*, *or* or *but* which joins two or more words (*cat and mouse*), groups, or clauses of equal status. It could link two nouns, like *than* in *I'd rather have an apple than a pear*. It could link two noun phrases, like *yet* in *It is completely waterproof, yet light and comfortable*. It could link two clauses, like *but* in *I want to use my bike, but I think that the front tyre is flat*.

There are two negative co-ordinating conjunctions, *neither* and *nor*: *The professor spoke neither English nor French.* The first of these may be used on its own, but not the latter, which now is always part of the neither ... nor construction: *Neither of them knew the way to the party* or *Neither he nor she knew the way to the party.* The use of *nor* on its own is now part of literary history: *Nor he nor she knew the way to the party.*

A **subordinating conjunction**, such as *although*, *because*, *why* or *when*, joins a dependent or subordinate clause to a main verb: *We asked her why she had left.* The expression *why she had left* is a subordinate clause, and thus *why* is a subordinating conjunction; *see also* **subordinate** *or* **dependent clause**.

connective *or* **connector**: an item that links linguistic units, such as conjunctions and certain adverbs, e.g. *moreover*.

connotation: an association, either personal or emotional, that is implied by a word.

consonance: the recurrence of similar-sounding consonants in the same position in a sequence of words, giving harmony; *compare with* **dissonance**.

consonant: a speech sound in which the breath is at least partly obstructed, and which to form a syllable must be combined with a vowel.

constituent: a linguistic unit that is an element of a larger construction.

content word *or* **lexical word**: a word that has a dictionary meaning of its own.

context: the parts of something written or spoken that immediately preceed and follow a word or passage and clarify its meaning.

continuant: a speech sound in which the vocal tract is only partly closed, allowing the breath to pass through and the sound to be prolonged, as with *f, r, s, v.*

continuous tenses: *see* **tense,** *also* **future continuous, future perfect progressive** *or* **future perfect continuous, future time, past perfect progressive, past progressive, present perfect progressive, present progressive.**

contraction: the shortening of a word by either combination or elision: *I am* contracts to *I'm.*

convergence: the gradual process of linguistic change in which dialects become more alike.

conversational analysis: analysis of the methods used when presenting or responding to ideas and information by means of the spoken word.

conversational maxims: the general principles for the efficient use of language, such as clarity, economy and relevance of speech and meaning.

conversion: a word that can exist in more than one word class without the addition of an affix, e.g. *slum* which can be either a noun or a verb.

co-ordination: the harmonious or effective linking of linguistic units having the same grammatical status, e.g. two noun phrases: *the belt and the braces.*

copula, copular verb: *see* **linking verb.**

co-reference: an element that requires reference to another element in the text for interpretation.

corpus: a collection of writings, texts, spoken material amassed for linguistic evaluation.

correctness: the absolute standard of language use.

correlative: pairs or sets of words that correspond to, and imply, each other without necessarily mentioning both, as in *cause* and *effect.*

countable noun *or* **count noun:** one which can be preceded by *a* and that can form a plural (as in *a book / books; a flower / flowers*); *see also* **uncountable noun.**

creole: a mother tongue that has been formed by the contact of a European language (often English, French or Portuguese) with another, especially African.

cryptography: the art of using codes and ciphers in writing a text which is intended to be secret.

cursive: writing done fluently, characterised by curved characters, rounded or flowing strokes.

dactyl: a unit of rhythm in poetic metre, consisting of one heavy (stressed) beat followed by two light (unstressed) beats.

dangling participle: one that has been misplaced in a sentence. A participle may be used to give impact, introducing a phrase which is attached to a subject mentioned later in a sentence: *Exhausted by the long journey, she fell on the bed in utter weariness.* The participle is *Exhausted* and *she* is the subject. It is a common error for such a participle not to be related to any subject, as in *Listening, there was much to interest the specialist and the layman alike.*

It is also a common error for a participle to be related to the wrong subject in a sentence: *Shaking the tree, some of the nuts fell on his head*, where *Shaking* is the participle and should go with a subject *he*. Instead it goes with *some of the nuts*. Participles in this situation are more properly known as misrelated participles, and may give the same unintentionally hilarious effects as the equally common misplaced **gerund**: *After fighting the flames for several hours, the ship was abandoned.*

dash: a punctuation mark (–) that typically indicates a short break in the continuity of a sentence: *He does not normally turn up on time –*

quite the opposite; *I was surprised they turned up together – I thought they weren't talking*. In such situations it may serve the same purpose as a **semicolon**, except that it is considered more informal.

Similarly it may be used twice in the same sentence, replacing a set of round brackets. A pair of dashes may be used to indicate an included unit in a sentence: *It was – after all – the most that we could expect*.

The dash should be used sparingly, in order to avoid carelessly writing down ideas as they occur rather than fashioning them into a piece of coherent prose. It may be used to emphasise a word or phrase: *They left holding hands – tightly*. It can also be used to add a remark to the end of a sentence: *They left the best of friends – not something that we had ever expected to happen*. It may also be used to introduce a statement that amplifies or explains what has been said: *The children ate everything that was in the fridge – the cakes, the yoghurt, the jelly, the ice cream, the strawberries and even the tomatoes*; it can be used to summarise what has gone before: *Mumps, measles and chickenpox – these were the major childhood illnesses before reliable vaccination programmes were introduced*.

The dash is also used to introduce an afterthought: *You should take this one – if it fits*. It may also introduce a sharp change of subject: *Oh good! here's the milkman – what did you say?*. It can also be used in order to introduce some kind of balance in a sentence: *It'll need both of us to wrap these presents – one to hold down the knots and one to tie them tightly*.

Dashes are used to indicate hesitant speech: *I*

can't – well – maybe – perhaps I can. They can be used to indicate the omission of part of a word or name: *It was Mr J– who told me*.

They can also be used between points in time or space: *1914–18* and *New York–London*.

dates: usually written in figures, as *1066*, rather than in words, as in *ten sixty-six*, except in formal contexts such as legal documents. The standard form in Britain is traditionally the day followed by the month followed by the year (*10 July 1944*), whereas in America the standard form of the same date is *July 10 1944*. This is also acceptable in Britain, and is becoming more common with the widespread adoption of American computer software. Care should be taken when writing dates entirely in numbers, especially if one is corresponding with someone in America. In Britain and in America the same sequence is used as for the spelt-out form, so that whereas an English person would more naturally write *10 / 7 / 44* for *10 July 1944*, an American would interpret this numerical form as *7 October 1944*.

Another accepted form is *10th July, 1944* in Britain, although now the comma is usually omitted. Centuries may be written either in figures (*the 19th century*) or in words (*the nineteenth century*). Decades and centuries in their numerical form are now usually written without apostrophes, as in *1950s*.

dative case: the Latin case which is translated as *to* or *for* in English, where such meanings are expressed by prepositional phrases. In English the indirect object is equivalent to the dative case in some situations.

deca~: a prefix derived from Greek and meaning

ten: *decade*, *decagon*, *decahedron* and *decalitre*.

deci~: a prefix derived from Latin and meaning *one-tenth*: *decibel*, *decimal*, *decigram* and *decimate*.

decibel: a unit (one-tenth of a bel) for measuring the relative intensity of sounds (symbol dB).

declarative question: used in informal speech, these are questions with the same word-order as declarative sentences, but they have a rising intonation, like questions. A declarative question can be used to ask for the confirmation of something that we think we know already: *That's the boss?* = *I suppose that's the boss, is it?*, or to express surprise: *THAT's the boss?* = *a funny little man like that?*.

declarative sentence: one which takes the form of a simple statement, and conveys information. The subject precedes the verb: *The wind blew*; *He has gone to another shop*; *The dog barked*; *There is nobody here*.

declarative mood: *see* **indicative mood**.

declension: the variation in the form of a noun, adjective or pronoun by which its grammatical case, number and gender are identified. It was part of the grammar of Latin and of other languages derived from it, but is not used in English.

decode: to convert a secret message or obscurely-worded text into plain and intelligible language.

defective: words that do not have all of the usual inflections, such as auxiliary verbs, which lack the usual verb inflections.

defining relative clause, **identifying relative clause** *or* **restrictive relative clause:** cannot be omitted from the sentence, because it defines the noun it is related to. In *Is that the woman who wants to buy your car?*, the question *Is that the woman?*

makes no sense on its own without the relative clause. In *The box on the right has got biscuits in*, the relative clause *on the right* is equally essential.

A defining relative clause is is not separated from the rest of the sentence, for example by commas: *The woman who cuts my hair has moved to another hairdresser's*. When a relative clause is separated by commas it is commenting, not defining: *My son, whose birthday it is today, will be joining us for lunch*.

We often use the relative pronoun *that* in defining relative clauses if the style is informal, instead of the other relative pronouns: *Where's the girl that (who) sells the tickets?*; *He's a man that (whom) people like at first sight*.

The relative pronoun can be left out if it is the object of the verb (or the object of the preposition following the verb) in the defining relative clause: *He's a man [whom / that] people like at first sight*, where *[whom / that]* would be the object of the verb *like*.

If the style is formal, prepositions may be put before the relative pronoun in a defining relative clause: *The people with whom he worked regarded him as eccentric*, the preposition *with* appears before the relative pronoun *whom*. In a more informal style, this sentence becomes *The people he worked with thought he was a bit strange*; the relative pronoun has been left out because it is the object of the preposition *with*.

Present and past tenses are used in defining relative clauses even where logic might demand the future or conditional. The sentence *I'll give you anything you ask for* reads far more smoothly than *you will ask for*; similarly in *I would never do anything that went against my conscience, that*

would go would be even more effortful ; *see also*
object, **relative clause**.

definite article: in English *the*, which is the most
frequently used word in the English language. It
may be used to make a general statement about
all things of a particular type: *The aeroplane has
made travel easier*; *The car has caused a lot of
laziness*. It may be used to refer to a whole class
or group: *the teachers*, *the Headteachers* and *the
university students*. It may also be used to refer
to services or systems: *He never uses the phone*.
Similarly it can be used to refer to a musical
instrument: *I never learnt to play the piano*.

The may indicate that a person or thing is the
only one: *the Bible*; *the King of Spain*; *the White
House*; *the President of the United States*. It may
be used instead of a possessive determiner to
refer to parts of the body: *He led her by the arm*;
She slapped him on the back. It is used in front of
superlative adjectives: *the tallest building in the
world*; *the most expensive ring in the shop*. It can
also be used to indicate that a person or thing is
unique or exceptional: *the scientific genius of the
century*. In this last sense *the* may be pronounced
thee, and written in italics to show the emphasis:
'Dior was *the* couture designer after the War'.
The is used to refer back to a person or thing that
has already been mentioned: *Anne ordered a cake.
The cake was the biggest she could afford*; *I bought
a cake. It was the cheapest [cake] I could find.*

degree: the level of comparison of gradable
adjectives. The degrees of comparison in
English comprise **positive** (*cold, hot, dark, fair,
short* and *tall*); **comparative** (*colder, hotter, darker,
fairer, shorter* and *taller*); **superlative** (*coldest,
hottest, darkest, fairest, shortest* and *tallest*).

In exactly the same way, degree can also refer to adverbs. Adverbs of degree include *extremely, greatly, rather, really, remarkably, slightly, somewhat, terribly, very: an extremely rare stamp; a greatly improved service; a rather odd couple; it's not really dark yet; he's remarkably stupid; this print is slightly foxed; the weather is somewhat cold; she's terribly pretty; a very old man*).

deixis: elements, including personal pronouns, demonstrative adverbs, adjectives and pronouns, that point directly to the personal aspect, time or place in speaking or writing: *he, then, there*.

deletion: the omission of an element of sentence structure: in *I said I was ready, that* is omitted.

demi~: a prefix derived from old French and meaning *half, half-sized, partially* or *imperfectly*, as in *demi-semiquaver*.

demonstrative determiner: used to indicate the person or thing in relationship to the speaker or writer in space or time. *This* and *these* indicate nearness to the speaker: *Will you take this CD back to the shop?; These grapes are for you. That* and *those* indicate distance from the speaker: *Get that dog out of here!; Aren't those puppies in the window beautiful!.*

demonstrative pronoun: similar to demonstrative determiners, except that they stand alone in place of a noun rather than preceding one: *I'm very grateful for this; Whatever can that be?; These are new proposals; Those are not my gloves.*

dependent clause: *see* **subordinate clause**.

derivation: has two meanings. It can refer to the tracing of the origin of a word: *The derivation is from the original Old High German*. It can also refer to the process of forming a new word by adding an affix of some kind to an existing word or base, as for example *action* from *act*, *helpless* from *help*.

derivative: refers to a word formed by derivation; for example, *quickly* is a derivative of *quick*.

derm~: an affix derived from Greek and meaning *skin*, as in *dermatitis*, *dermatology* and *pachyderm*.

descender: the part of a letter that projects below the foot of the lower-case *x* (the *baseline*).

determiner: a word used in front of a noun or pronoun to tell us something about it. They are divided into the following five categories:

- articles *a*, *an*, *the*: *a camel*, *an elephant*, *the desert*.
- demonstrative determiners *this*, *that*, *these*, *those*: *this hat*, *that coat*, *these shoes*, *those shirts*.
- possessive determiners *my*, *your*, *his / her / its*, *our*, *their*: *my house*, *your dog*, *his briefcase*, *her handbag*, *its foodbowl*, *our flat*, *their liability*.
- cardinal numbers e.g. *one*, *two*, *three* and ordinal numbers e.g. *first*, *second*, *third*: *one door*; *two rooms*; *first day*; *second night*.
- indefinite or general determiners *all*, *another*, *any*, *both*, *each*, *either*, *enough*, *every*, *few*, *fewer*, *less*, *little*, *many*, *most*, *much*, *neither*, *no*, *other*, *several*, *some*: *all children*; *another helping*; *any day*; *both parents*; *each applicant*; *either alternative*; *many mothers*; *some teachers*.

Many words used as determiners can also be pronouns; *see* **adjective**; **demonstrative determiner**; **indefinite pronoun**; **number**; **personal pronoun**.

deviance: failure to conform to the rules of language.

di~: a prefix derived from Greek and meaning *two* as in *dichord*, *dilemma*, *dioxide*; *twice* as in *dibranchiate*, *dibutyl*; or *double* as in *dicentra*, *diene*.

dia~: a prefix derived from Greek and meaning *through* as in *dianoetic*, *diaspora*; *apart* as in *diapason*, *diapophysis*; or *across* as in *diameter*.

diachronic linguistics: *see* **historical linguistics**.

diacritic: a sign, such as an accent, diaeresis, or cedilla, used to indicate a different sound or value for that particular letter.

diaeresis: a mark placed over a vowel to indicate that it is sounded separately from a neighbouring vowel, as in *naïve*. They are omitted in America.

diagramming: *see* **parsing**.

dialect: a subordinate variety of language that is distinct from other varieties in terms of its vocabulary, pronunciation, accent or grammar. The term implies a deviation from the standard form of a language, such as the Queen's or standard English, or received pronunciation.

At one time regional dialects were considered to be a sign of a lack of education, as demonstrated in the writings of Thomas Hardy. Even until relatively recently, people with regional accents or using local dialects were unlikely to get jobs in radio or television, where the clarity of language is important in reaching the widest possible audience. Those pursuing such careers tried to modify or even to lose their accents, but since the advent of regional television and local radio stations, presenters have been positively encouraged to use regional accents.

Dialects tend to be peculiar to a particular region, so that there is a Newcastle dialect, a Glasgow dialect, and so on. Alternatively, they may be based on class differences, when they are sometimes known as social dialects. Upper-middle-class dialect is the basis for standard English, whereas the demotic 'estuary' English now incorporates usage and intonation from a wide variety of sources, such as Australian soap opera, absorbed from the popular media.

The word *dialect* is not appropriate if one is referring to a variety of English that is spoken in another country; the form spoken in America is known as American English.

dialect continuum *or* **dialect chain:** a chain of dialects spoken within the same geographical region; the local area in which each dialect is spoken cannot be easily distinguished from the others.

dialectology *or* **dialect geography:** the study of dialects, especially with reference to regional dialects.

dialogue: conversation in written form. In novels it is placed on a new line, often in a new paragraph, if there is a change of speaker:

'Hand me that box down', said her uncle. 'No!, not that one, the one on the left, and be careful'.
'Why, what's in it?' enquired Jane.

Plays are written almost entirely in dialogue, apart from stage directions; they have no narrative as such.

diction: the pronunciation and enunciation of words in speaking and singing, with regard to correctness, clarity and precision. It can also refer to the effective choice of words in writing or speech.

digraph: a group of two letters that together represent one sound: *ay* in *stay*, *ey* in *key*, *oy* in *ploy*, *ph* in *pharmacy* and *th* in *thick*; *see* **ligature**.

dimeter: a line of verse containing two units of rhythm.

diminutive: something implying smallness, or a small form or version of something: *booklet, droplet, duckling, flatlet, gosling, hillock, islet, kitchenette, majorette, piglet, snippet, starlet.* Proper names often have diminutive forms, which imply affection and familiarity: *Al* for

Alan, *Ben* for Benedict or Benjamin, *Chas* for Charles, *Fi* for Fiona, *Beth* or *Liz* for Elizabeth, *Gill* for Gillian, *Hal* or *Harry* for Henry, *Jim* for James, *Bel* for Isabel, *Mick* or *Mike* for Michael, *Pat* or *Trish* for Patricia, *Tom* for Thomas, *Bill* or *Will* for William.

diphthong *or* **gliding vowel:** a speech sound in one syllable in which the articulation begins as for one vowel and moves towards another. Examples include the vowel sounds in *aisle, coin, either, height, house, know, loud, rain, road, soul, voice, weigh,* and *weird.* Since the sound glides from one vowel into another, a diphthong is sometimes called a gliding vowel.

diphthongisation: the adding of a diphthongal quality to what was formerly a pure vowel.

directive: *see* **command**.

direct object: the primary object of the action of a transitive verb. It is the noun group which is used to refer to someone or something directly affected by or involved in the action performed by the subject.

A direct object can be a noun, and in the sentence *Mary hit the ball, the ball* is the object. In the sentence *They bought a house, the house* is the object. In the sentence *You made an error, an error* is the object.

A **noun phrase** can be a direct object, and in the sentence *He has bought a large house, a large house* is the object. In the sentence *She loves the little girl, the little girl* is the object. In the sentence *They both wear the company uniform, the company uniform* is the object.

A direct object can be a **subordinate clause**, and in the sentence *I know what he means, what he means* is the object. In the sentence *He denied* *that he had been involved*, *that he had been involved* is the object. In the sentence *I asked when he would return*, *when he would return* is the object.

A direct object can also be a pronoun, and in the sentence *She hit him*, *him* is the object. In the sentence *They had a car but they sold it*, *it* is the object. In the sentence *She loves them*, *them* is the object; *see* **object**; **indirect object**.

direct speech: reporting of speech by repeating exactly the actual words used by the speaker. In the sentence *'What was in it?' I asked*, the question *'What was in it?'* is a piece of direct speech because it represents exactly what I said. Similarly, in the sentence *'Because it is an utterly specious argument from beginning to end'*, *he answered* the reply *'Because it is an utterly specious argument from beginning to end'* is a piece of direct speech since it represents exactly what he said.

Quotation marks, also known as **inverted commas** or (informally) as **quotes**, are used at the beginning and the end of pieces of direct speech. Only the words and punctuation actually spoken are placed within the quotation marks, as in *'It is a most tragic story'*, *I agreed, 'but why have you not carried out his wishes?'* The quotation marks used may be either single or double, according to preference or house style. If there is a statement such as *I said* following the piece of direct speech, a comma is placed after the second quotation mark, as in *'A fine day indeed'*, *she agreed*. However, if the speech is continued after a pause, as in *'My dear Erskine,' I responded, 'I am so sorry to have put you to such trouble'*, the comma belongs within the quotation marks because it is part of the speech being quoted. Question or exclamation marks may be used as appropriate instead of the comma, as in *'Dead!' I shrieked*.

When a statement such as *I said* is placed within a sentence of direct speech, the second part of the piece of direct speech does not begin with a capital letter unless it begins a new sentence: *'Fermat,' I murmured, 'it is your duty to give this theorem to the world.'* If the piece of direct speech begins a sentence, the sentence begins with a capital letter: *He said 'You have been carried away by the sentiment of the whole story.'* The full stop at the end of a whole sentence of direct speech should go before the closing quotation mark. If the piece of direct speech quoted takes up more than one paragraph, quotation marks are placed at the beginning of each new paragraph. However, quotation marks are not placed at the end of each paragraph, only at the end of the final one.

Quotation marks are not used only to indicate direct speech. For example, they are sometimes used to indicate the title of a book, magazine or newspaper, the name of a ship or title of a play. The quotation marks used in this way can be either single or double, according to preference or house style. If a piece of direct speech contains the title of a book etc, it should be put in the opposite type of quotation marks to those used to enclose the piece of direct speech. Thus, if single quotation marks have been used in the direct speech, then double quotation marks should be used for the title within the direct speech: *'Have you read "The Ballad of Reading Gaol" by Oscar Wilde?' asked the librarian*. If double quotation marks have been used for the direct speech, single quotation marks should be used for the title: *"Have you read 'The Ballad of Reading Gaol' by Oscar Wilde?" asked the librarian*. Alternatively, the book title may be italicised instead of appearing within any quotation marks at all, following the trend to use less punctuation but still distinguishing it from the surrounding text. Where italics are used for the surrounding text, the title would then be in normal roman type; either 'Have you read *The Ballad of Reading Gaol* by Oscar Wilde?' or *Have you read* The Ballad of Reading Gaol *by Oscar Wilde?* is clear.

dis~: a prefix derived from Latin and expressing negation (*dishonest*); reversal or absence of an action or state (*disengage, disbelieve*); indicating removal of a thing or quality (*distinguish, dispose*); completeness of action (*disembowel, disgruntled*) or expulsion from (*disbar*).

discontinuous: the splitting of a grammatical construction by the insertion of another unit (*Turn the sound down*).

discourse: a continuous stretch of language, longer than a sentence, often used in an academic context or of an exposition of a specialised subject.

discourse analysis: the study of patterns of linguistic organisation in discourses.

disjunction: a statement expressing the relationship of two mutually incompatible alternatives: *Either he's already left or he hasn't arrived yet*.

dissimilation: the influence that sound segments have upon each other, so that they become less alike (as in *cinnamon*, originally *cinnamom*).

dissonance: the use of sounds to convey unpleasant effects.

distribution: the total set of linguistic environments in which an element of language can occur.

distributive pronoun: refers to individual members of a class or group. The group includes *each*, *either*, *neither*, *none*, *everyone*, *no-one*. Such pronouns take singular verbs and singular personal pronouns: *Emma, Lucy and Andrea have worked hard this year; each has passed her exams.*

Problems arise when the gender of the noun to which the distributive pronoun refers back is either unknown or unspecified (*see* **dual gender**). It used to be the convention to treat such nouns as masculine and so to make the distributive pronoun masculine: *The students have been advised by their professor that each is to produce his essay by tomorrow.* This convention is now regarded as unacceptably sexist; one solution is to use *him / her* (or *him or her*), as in *The students have been advised by their professor that each is to produce his or her essay by tomorrow.* However, this is undeniably clumsy and has given rise to the ungrammatical use of a plural personal pronoun, as in *The students have been advised by their professor that each is to produce their essay by tomorrow.* It is preferable to rephrase sentences to avoid these pitfalls: *All the students have been advised by their professor to produce their essays by tomorrow.* Pronouns such as *each* and *either* here are fairly formal; in less formal situations *each of* or *either of* would be more usual: *Each of the players will have to train late tonight; Either of the keys will fit the lock.*

disyllabic: a word with two syllables; for example, *pardon* is disyllabic, since it consists of the syllable *par* and the syllable *don*.

ditransitive: said of verbs which take two objects.

do: an auxiliary verb which is used to form negative forms: *I do not want to go*; *They don't always go*; *She didn't approve of their going.*

It is also used to form interrogative forms: *Do you want to?*; *Does she know you want to?*; *Did you know that?*; *He prefers to go later. Don't you?.*

Do is also used for emphasis: *I do think that's awful*; *They do know about it, don't they?.*

~dom: a suffix meaning state, condition (*freedom*). It can also mean rank or status (*earldom*), domain (*kingdom*), or a category of people regarded collectively (*officialdom*).

dorsal: sounds that are made with the back of the tongue.

double negative: statement containing two negative elements (*I didn't have nothing*).This is usually considered incorrect in standard English, although it is a feature of some social or regional dialects. The use of the double negative, if taken literally, has the opposite meaning to the one intended; thus *I didn't have nothing* means that actually I had something.

Some double negatives are considered acceptable (*I shouldn't be surprised if he didn't take it*), although it is better to restrict such constructions to informal contexts.

double passive: refers to a clause which contains two verbs in the passive, the second of which is an infinitive (as in *The books are expected to be returned later this week*). They are often clumsy or ungrammatical and should be avoided.

doubles *or* **dyads:** words habitually associated with each other: *black and white, fair and square, give and take, hale and hearty, high and dry, hue and cry, in and out, rough and ready, stuff and nonsense, ups and downs, wear and tear.*

doublets: pairs of words that have developed from the same original word, but have evolved separately to differ somewhat in form and, usually, in meaning. Examples include *cloak* and *clock*, *fashion* and *faction*, *frail* and *fragile*, *human* and *humane*, *shade* and *shadow*.

doubling of consonants: there are few rules in English grammar, but one that does help with spelling is that, in words of one syllable ending in a single consonant preceded by a single vowel, the consonant is doubled when an ending starting with a vowel is added: *stop* and *stopped*, *bat* and *batting*. In words of more than one syllable that end in a single consonant preceded by a single vowel, the consonant is doubled if the stress is on the last syllable: *propel* and *propelling*, *prefer* and *preferred* and *commit* and *committal*. In similar words where the stress is not on the last syllable, the consonant does not double: *pallet* and *palletised*, *pander* and *pandering*, *proffer* and *profferer*.

    Exceptions to this rule include words ending in *l*. The *l* doubles, even in cases where the last syllable containing it is unstressed (as in *compel* and *compellable*, *rebel* and *rebellion*). *Worship*, in which the stress is on the first syllable, is also an exception, which is developed into *worshipped*.

dramatic irony: a situation in which a character in a play or novel says or does something that has a meaning for the audience or reader, other than the obvious meaning, that the character does not understand. Its use is common in both comedy and tragedy.

dual alphabet: the use of capital and small letters in a single system. Modern European languages use both capitals and lower-case, although

Latin used only capitals; lower-case letters
came later.

dual gender: a category of nouns in which there is
no indication of gender, i.e. they may be either
male or female. Unless the gender is specified
we do not know the sex of the person referred to.
They comprise a range of words used for people,
and occasionally animals, including *artist*,
author, *bird*, *child*, *cook*, *musician*, *neighbour*,
parent, *player*, *poet*, *pupil*, *scientist*, *singer*,
student, *teacher*, *worker*. Even forms such as
manageress, *sculptress* and so on have fallen out
of general use, giving rise to problems with
accompanying singular pronouns; *see* **each**, **~ess**.

dummy subject: describes a subject that has no
intrinsic meaning but is inserted to maintain a
balanced grammatical structure. In the sentence
It is beginning to get dark, the pronoun *it* is a
dummy subject. In the sentence *There is nothing
left to eat*, the pronoun *there* is a dummy subject.

duration: the length of time involved in the
articulation of a sound or syllable.

dyads: *see* **doubles**.

dynamic verb: refers to a verb with a meaning that
indicates action, for example *walk* in *They will
have to walk home*.

dys~: a prefix derived from the Greek and
meaning *bad* or *ill*: *dysfunctional*, *dysphonia*,
dysphoria, *dyslexia*, *dystrophy*.

dyslexia: a development disorder that affects the
ability to read and spell, which until very
recently was often undiagnosed. There is an
analagous disorder with respect to numbers and
their sequence.

dysphemism: a use of a language that emphasises
unpleasantness: *a foul filthy stench*.

each: may be either a determiner or a distributive pronoun, and in both cases it refers to the individuals within a group, not the group itself.

When used as a determiner, it preceeds a singular noun and takes a singular verb: *Each child is to dance in turn*; *Each parent has to buy a ticket*; *Each school is represented by a maths teacher*.

The quantifier *each of* followed by the article *the* may sometimes be substituted for *each* if the latter is a determiner: *Each of the children*. Here again a singular verb is used: *Each of the parents has to buy a ticket*.

Each of may also be used before plural pronouns (*each of them*), when again a singular verb is used: *Each of them has to buy a ticket*.

If the user wishes to emphasise the fact that something is true about every member of a group, *each one of* can be used: *Each one of us must buy a ticket*.

As a pronoun *each* also takes a singular verb: *Each is watching the other*. *Each one* can be used for emphasis: *Each one is represented by a maths teacher*.

The determiner and pronoun *each*, where relevant, should be accompanied by a singular personal pronoun: *Each girl has to dance on her own*; *Each horse has eaten all of its hay*.

When the noun that each refers back to is of unknown or unspecified gender, political correctness now demands the abandonment of the former convention that, where necessary, the masculine includes the feminine: *Each pupil is required to bring his own music* and *Each of the teachers has to provide himself with a score* must be modified by the use of *he or her*, *his or her*. These examples then become *Each pupil is* required to bring his or her own music; *Each of the teachers has to provide himself or herself with a score card*). In written English this is dull as well as clumsy, and it sounds even more pedestrian when spoken. For this reason ungrammatical usage (*Each pupil is required to bring their own music*; *Each of the teachers has to provide themselves with a score*) is becoming increasingly prevalent.

Sexism and grammatical error alike may be avoided by rephrasing such sentences (*All pupils are required to bring their own music*; *All of the teachers have to provide themselves with a score*).

Each is used rather than *every* when the user is thinking of the members of a group as individuals.

echo utterance: speech which repeats, in whole or in part, what has just been said by another speaker.

eco~: a prefix used in forming words that describe something related to ecology. Increased awareness of the importance of the environment has fostered interest in ecology and many words beginning with *eco~* have been added to the English language. Some of these are scientific terms such as *ecosystem*, while others are more general. Contemporary usage has coined such useful terms as *eco-friendly*, *eco-politics*, *eco-terrorism*, and *eco-warrior*; others, more derogatory in tone such as *ecofreak* and *econut*, should be regarded as slang.

~ectomy: a suffix derived from Greek and meaning *to cut out*. It thus indicates a surgical operation in which part of the body is removed, such as *hysterectomy*, the surgical removal of the womb.

~ed: a suffix which forms the past tense and past

participles of regular verbs (*aimed*, *baked*, *called*, *depended*, *expected*, *failed*, *guessed*, *harmed*, *indicated*, *jailed*, *kissed*, *lamented*, *marvelled*, *noticed*, *operated*, *pointed*, *questioned*, *related*, *snorted*, *trembled*, *unveiled*, *varnished*, *waited*, *X-rayed*, *yawned*, *zigzagged*).

Some past participles ending in ~*ed* can act as adjectives, as in *escaped animals.*

In the case of some verbs, the past tense and past participle may end in ~*ed* or ~*t*, according to preference. e.g. *burn* (*burned* and *burnt*), *dream* (*dreamed* and *dreamt*), *learn* (*learned* and *learnt*) are acceptable forms. However, although in England they are more or less interchangeable or depend on context or style, in American English the ~*t* form is very rare.

~**ee:** a suffix derived from French, used in the formation of nouns denoting the person affected by the verbal action (*addressee*, *divorcee*, *employee*). It may be used also of a person concerned with or described as (*absentee* and *refugee*), or be used to describe an object of smaller size (*bootee*). It is frequently wrongly used, for example *attendee*, meaning someone who has attended a meeting or intends to do so, when *attender*, *delegate* or *participant* would be both clearer and more correct. Thus does our language become corrupt and impoverished.

e.g.: the abbreviation of the Latin phrase *exempli gratia*, meaning *for example*. It is used in giving examples of what has previously been referred to: *The children wanted to see some of the animals in the zoo, e.g. elephants, penguins and seals, at feeding time.* By its very nature, e.g. is mostly restricted to written English, becoming *for example* in speech. Many writers also prefer to use *for example* rather than the Latin abbreviation.

Both letters of the abbreviation usually have a full stop after them, as e.g., and it is usually preceded by a comma.

either: may be used as a co-ordinating conjunction, a pronoun, a quantifier or a determiner.

It is used as a co-ordinating conjunction with the other additional conjunction *or*. In this construction, a singular verb is used if both subjects are singular: *Either my mother or my father knows the way.* A plural verb is used if both nouns involved are plural: *Teams of either boys or girls are allowed to use the ground for organised sports.* When a combination of singular and plural subjects is involved, the verb traditionally agrees with the subject which is nearer to it: *Either my parents or my brother will give you a lift.*

As a distributive pronoun, *either* is used to refer to one of two things, people, or situations, to say that they are both possible and it does not matter which one is chosen: *There were glasses of well-iced champagne and canapes. Very few of either were left after the reception.* It takes a singular verb if there is only one item in each alternative: *We have visited both schools and either is suitable.*

Either is followed by *of* when used as a quantifier before a plural noun: *either of the days*; *either of the dishes*. It takes a singular verb: *either of the days is suitable*; *either of the dishes will be deep enough for the fruit.*

It is used with a singular verb as a determiner: *either way is possible.*

electro~: a prefix meaning related to, or caused by, electricity (*electrocute, electrode, electromagnet*).

electropalatograph: an instrument which records the contacts made between the tongue and the palate during speech.

elision: the omission of a speech sound or syllable in connected speech, as in *I'm*, *let's*, *e'en*.

ellipsis: an omission of some kind. Usually it refers to the omission of words from a sentence because they are thought to be obvious from the context. In many cases an auxiliary verb is used on its own rather than a full verb, as in *He doesn't like it but I do*, where the full form of *He doesn't like it but I do like it* would sound unnatural and repetitive. This is common in spoken English.

Some ellipses sound clumsy as well as ungrammatical: *Mine is as big, or perhaps even bigger than, yours*, where *as* is omitted after *big*. Care should be taken to avoid ellipsis which might give rise to ambiguity.

An ellipsis is often used in printed matter to indicate an omission from a quoted passage. In quoting a long passage only the beginning and ending phrases are used, separated by three closely-spaced dots (...). If the part of the passage quoted does not start at the beginning of a sentence, three dots also precede it; if the quotation ends before the sentence being quoted, the ellipsis is used instead of a full stop.

elocution: the art of clear and expressive speech, especially of distinct pronunciation and articulation when applied to public speaking.

embedding: the insertion of one grammatical unit within another, such as *who scored* in *The player who scored was a substitute.*

emphasising adjective: an adjective used for emphasis, such as *very* in *His very existence makes me shiver*).

emphasising adverb: an adverb used for emphasis,

such as *really* in *I really don't care whether you go or stay*.

emphatic pronoun: a reflexive pronoun that is used for emphasis: *She knows herself that it will never be allowed*.

empty word *or* **prop word:** a meaningless word that expresses a grammatical relationship, such as *It* in *It's today that he gets his new car*.

en~: a prefix meaning *causing to be* (*enlarge*, *enrich*, *enslave*), and *putting into or onto* (*enfold*, *endanger*, *engulf*, *entangle*, *entrust*).

~en: a suffix with several functions. It may mean *causing to be* (*darken*, *sweeten*, *widen*). It also indicates a diminutive or small version (*kitten*), and what something is made of (*wooden*, *woollen*), and to form the past participle of many irregular words (*broken*, *drunken*, *fallen*, *taken*).

encode: to convert a message from one system into another code or cipher system.

ending: the final part, consisting of an inflection, which is added to a base or root word. The *~er* of *poorer* is an ending, as is the *~ly* of *poorly*.

enjambment: the running on of a sentence without a pause beyond the end of a line, couplet, or stanza.

entry word: *see* **headword**.

epenthesis: the insertion of a letter or sound in the middle of a word, such as *b* in *thimble*.

epic: originally a long narrative poem relating the heroic deeds and adventures of legendary figures, the most important examples being the *Iliad* and *Odyssey* by Homer. In modern usage it has been extended to include novels or films that are based on an epic narrative or are heroic in type or scale; it is misused to convey *lengthy*.

epigram: a figure of speech consisting of a brief,

pointed and witty poem, saying or maxim, for example *A man who knows the price of everything and the value of nothing*. This was the reply by Lord Darlington to Cecil Graham's question *What is a cynic?* in Act III, *Lady Windermere's Fan*, by Oscar Wilde. Many of the best-known epigrams are by Wilde or by George Bernard Shaw.

epigraph: an inscription that appears on stone buildings, statues, coins; also, a phrase or quotation on the title page or chapter opening of a book.

epigraphy: the study of inscriptions, especially ancientones, and their interpretation.

epithet: an adjective that describes a quality or attribute of a noun, especially used with or as a name with which it is regularly associated (as in *Alfred the Great, have a nice day*).

eponym: refers to a person, real or imaginary, after whom something is named.

The name of the thing in question may also be referred to as an eponym, or it can be said to be eponymous, eponymous being the adjective from eponym. English has a number of eponymous words, some of which are listed below together with their derivations.

Cardigan, a knitted jacket fastened with buttons, called after the Earl of Cardigan (1797–1868) who was fond of wearing such a garment. He was the British cavalry officer who led the unsuccessful Charge of the Light Brigade during the Crimean War (1854).

Celsius, the temperature scale called after the Swedish astronomer, Anders Celsius (1701–44).

Leotard, a one-piece, close-fitting garment worn by acrobats and dancers, called after the

French acrobat, Jules Leotard (1842–70), who introduced it as a circus costume.

Mackintosh, a type of raincoat, especially one made of rubberised cloth, called after the Scottish chemist, Charles Mackintosh (1766–1843), who patented it in the early 1820s.

Maverick, an independent person who refuses to conform, called after the American pioneer Samuel Augustus Maverick (1803–70), who refused to brand his calves.

Pavlova, a meringue topped with cream and fruit, called after the Russian ballerina Anna Pavlova (1885–1931). The dessert was concocted by Australian chefs to celebrate her popularity during a tour of Australia and New Zealand.

Plimsoll, a type of light rubber-soled canvas shoe, called after the English shipping reform leader, Samuel Plimsoll (1824–98). The shoe is so named because the upper edge of the rubber was thought to resemble the Plimsoll Line, the set of markings on the side of a ship which indicate the levels to which the ship may be safely loaded. The Plimsoll Line became law in 1876.

Romeo, a lovelorn person, called after the character in *Romeo and Juliet* by William Shakespeare.

Sandwich, a snack consisting of two pieces of buttered bread with a filling, supposedly called after the Earl of Sandwich (1718–92) who was such a compulsive gambler that he would not leave the gaming tables to eat, but had brought to him some cold beef between two slices of bread.

Saxophone, a type of keyed brass instrument often used in jazz music, called after Adolphe (or Antoine-Joseph) Sax (1814–94), the Belgium instrument-maker who invented it.

Scrooge, a mean person, called after the character in *A Christmas Carol* by Charles Dickens.

Teddy Bear, a soft toy in the shape of a bear, called after the American president Theodore Roosevelt (1858–1919). The usage emerged after a cartoon showed Roosevelt, whose nickname was Teddy and who was a known bear-hunter, sparing the life of a bear cub.

Volt, the unit of electrical potential difference and electromotive force, called after the Italian physicist Alessandro Volta (1745–1827), who invented the electric battery.

Wellington, a waterproof rubber boot that extends to the knee, called after the Duke of Wellington (1769–1852), who defeated Napoleon at Waterloo in 1815.

equative: a clause which indicates that one thing is equal to, or the same as, another. The verb *to be* is sometimes known as an equative verb because it links a subject and complement which are equal to each other: *Mr Smith is an ironmonger*. Here, *Mr Smith* and *ironmonger* refer to the same person. Other equative verbs include *appear*, *become*, *look*, *remain* and *seem* (*He appears to be a nice person*; *I become very hungry by mid-day*; *She looks a lot younger than she is*; *You remain here while I go to look*; *You seem to know what you're doing*). Such verbs are more often known as **copula verbs**; *see also* **linking verb**.

~er: a suffix with several functions. It may indicate a person, animal or thing that performs a specified action or activity as in *carer*, *carrier*, *cleaner*, *computer*. Some words in this category may also end in *~or*, such as *adviser / advisor*. It may also indicate a person who is concerned with a specific thing or subject (*geographer*, *lawyer*). It also indicates a thing which does something, such as a *cooker*, *mixer*, *printer*. It may also indicate the comparative form of an adjective (*darker*, *lighter*, *hotter*, *colder*, *older*, *younger*).

It may indicate a person belonging to a specific place or group: *Londoner*, *New Zealander*, *villager*. It can also indicate a person or thing that has a specific attribute or form: *first-rater*, *foreigner*, *free-wheeler*. It can also be used in slang formations where the root word is distorted, such as *soccer*, *rugger*. It may be used for forming iterative and frequentative verbs, as in *blunder*, *glimmer*. It may be used in law to form nouns that denote verbal action or a document effecting this, as in *cesser*, *disclaimer*, *misnomer*.

~ese: a suffix indicating *belonging to* or *coming from*, and is used to denote an inhabitant or the language of a country or city, as in *Chinese*, *Japanese*, *Milanese*. By extension it refers to words indicating some kind of jargon, such as *computerese* and *journalese*.

Esq.: an abbreviation for *Esquire*, which is a title that can be appended to a man's surname when no other form of address is used. It is mostly used in formal contexts. It may be used instead of *Mr* when addressing an envelope to a man, and it is usually spelt with a full stop, as in *William Brown, Esq.* Although it is often done, whether as a result of ignorance or the desire to exaggerate the man's status, it is technically incorrect to use this form of address to a man whose family is not entitled to bear arms.

~esque: a prefix of French origin which means *in the style of* or *resembling*, as in *grotesque*, *picturesque, Plateresque, romanesque, statuesque*.

~**ess:** a suffix which was formerly widely used to indicate the feminine form of a word, as in *actress* from *actor*; *lioness* from *lion*; *mayoress* from *mayor*; *sculptress* from *sculptor*. In many cases the supposedly male form, such as *author*, *editor*, *poet*, is now considered a neutral form and so is used of either a woman or a man. Some words ending in ~*ess* remain, such as *princess*, *heiress*, *hostess*. It may also be used to form abstract nouns from adjectives (*duress*).

~**est:** a suffix forming the superlative forms of adjectives (*hardest, highest, hottest, humblest*), and adverbs (*soonest*).

etc: abbreviation of the Latin phrase *et cetera*, meaning *and the rest, and similar things*. It is used at the end of lists to indicate that there exist other examples of the kind of thing that has just been named: *He bought socks, shoes, shirts, trousers, ties, etc*; *At the sports centre you can play tennis, squash, snooker, etc*.

ethnolinguistics: the study of language in relation to ethnic groups and behaviour.

~**ette:** a suffix indicating a diminutive or smaller version (*cigarette, kitchenette*). It may also indicate *imitation* (*flannelette, leatherette*), or *female* (*majorette, suffragette*). In this last sense it is may be used disparagingly, as in *hackette* – a derogatory word for a female journalist.

etymological fallacy: the view that an earlier or older meaning of a word is the correct one.

etymology: the study of the origins and history of the form and meaning of a word. In addition, it refers to an account or statement of the formation of a word or phrase. It is usual to include etymologies in larger dictionaries,

often at the end of each entry. These indicate
which language the relevant word has been
derived from, for example, whether it has come
from Old English, Latin, Greek, French,
German, Dutch, Spanish, etc. Alternatively
they indicate which person, place, etc, the word
has been named after. Some dictionaries also
include the date at which the relevant word
entered the English language; *see* **borrowing**.

Many words and phrases in the English
language are of unknown or uncertain origin. In
such cases much guesswork goes on and various
suggestions are put forward, most of which
cannot be proved.

euphemism: a term given to an expression that is a
vaguer, milder, more pleasant or indirect way of
saying something that might be thought to be
too unpleasant or offensive. English has a great
many euphemisms, often referring to physical
functions. Euphemisms range from the high-
flown (*to go to a better place* or *pass away* for *die*);
through the coy (*getting on a bit, not as young as
one used to be* for *old*; *expecting a happy event, in
the club* for *pregnant*; *to spend a penny, answer the
call of nature* for *to urinate*); to slang (*do away
with oneself, top oneself* for *suicide*) and the
overtly mealy-mouthed (*to let [someone] go,
dispense with [someone's] services* for *to dismiss*;
hanky panky, make love for *sexual intercourse*).
Some purport to be amusing (*in one's birthday
suit, in the buff* for *naked*), while the origin of
others is obscure (*one over the eight, three sheets
to the wind* for *drunk*).

Many of the expressions advocated for use when
referring to physical and mental disabilities in a
positive way are euphemisms. These include

differently abled for *disabled* and *optically challenged* for *blind*, when these expressions do not accurately reflect the degree of ability, or (like the first example) suggest capabilities which may not exist. Such expressions are themselves patronising because the people so described cannot hope to live up to them, and therefore they should be avoided.

euphony: a pleasing sequence of sounds.

Euro~: a prefix meaning either *relating to Europe* (*Eurovision*), but now more commonly *relating to the European Community* (as in *Eurocrat*).

every: a determiner used with a singular noun to indicate that all the members of a group are being referred to. It takes a singular verb (*Every worker has four weeks' holiday*). *Every* should also take a singular pronoun (*Every man has his job to do*). When the gender of the noun to which *every* refers is unknown or unspecified, the former convention of assuming such a noun to be masculine although including the feminine, and accordingly of using masculine pronouns (*Every worker is to behave himself properly*), is now regarded as sexist. To avoid this, *he or she*, *him or her*, *his or her* and *himself or herself* may be used. This can become clumsy and many prefer to be ungrammatical by using *they*, *them*, *their* and *themselves*, as in *Every worker is to behave themselves properly*. However, any sentences of this kind can be rephrased to avoid being either sexist or ungrammatical (*All workers are to behave themselves properly*).

everyone: a pronoun which takes a singular verb (*Everyone is expected to arrive on time*). In order to be grammatically correct it takes a singular personal pronoun and it is subject to the same rules and kind of treatment as every; *see* **every**.

ex~: a prefix used to form verbs meaning *out* or *forth* (*exclude, exit*), or *upward* (*extol*), or *thoroughly* (*excruciate*), or *to bring into a state of* (*exasperate*), or *to remove or rid from* (*expatriate, exonerate*). Also it can be used meaning *formerly* to form nouns from titles of office or status, (*ex-convict, ex-chairman, ex-president, ex-wife*), as a preposition describing the sale of goods (*ex-works*), and colloquially by itself as a noun when referring to a former spouse, as in *my ex*.

exclamation: a word, phrase or sentence with strong feeling called out, or a sudden wordless cry. It is indicated by an exclamation mark (!) at the end of the exclamation (*Help!, Ouch!, Well, I never!*).

An exclamatory question is a sentence that is interrogative in form but is an exclamation in meaning (*Well, would you believe it!*).

exclusive: the first person plural pronoun *we*, when it does not include the person being addressed.

exegesis: a critical explanation of a text, especially of scripture.

existential: a sentence affirming or implying existence, particularly in the context of the philosophy which emphasises the importance of the will and responsibility of the individual.

expansion: adding new elements to a construction without affecting its basic structure.

expletive: an oath or swear word as exclamation.

expression: a word or phrase treated as a unit.

expressive: a use of language that displays or affects a person's emotions (*I have wasted time, and now doth Time waste me*).

extension: the widening of the meaning of a word in historical linguistics.

extra~: a prefix meaning *outside* or *beyond*: *extradite, extragalatic, extrajudicial, extraneous, extraordinary*.

extraposition: moving an element to a position at one end of a sentence (as in *The sun sets at night / At night the sun sets*).

eye rhyme: a pair of words that seem to rhyme from their spelling, but have different pronunciations (as in *come / home*).

fable: a story, especially a supernatural one, not based on fact, that is intended to convey a moral lesson. Fables frequently feature animals as characters which speak and act like human beings. The most famous are the *Fables of Æsop* (620–560BC), a slave who was very deformed. His stories were compiled by Babrios, a Greek living in the Alexandrian age. His fables include *The Hare and the Tortoise* and *The Boy who Cried Wolf*.

false borrowing: an apparent **borrowing**, which is really a construct like *cul-de-sac* or **nom de plume**.

false friends: are words that have the same or similar forms in different languages but have different meanings in each. For example, the French word *abusif* and the English word *abusive* are false friends; *abusif* means *incorrect*, *illegal*, *unauthorised*, *excessive* not *abusive*. The French word *actuel* and the English *actual* are false friends; *actuel* means *present-day* not *actual*. The Italian *eventuale* and the English *eventual* are false friends; *eventuale* means *possible* not *eventual*.

family: a group of languages, all of which ultimately derive from a single early language.

feedback: information about reactions to a piece of writing or a performance, which helps its creator to evaluate the efficiency of the communication of the writing or interpretation.

feminine: of or denoting the gender proper to female persons or animals. It is the opposite of *masculine*. The feminine gender demands the use of the appropriate pronoun, including *she*, *her*, *hers* and *herself*: *The girl wanted to go to town but she did not have the bus fare*.

feminine forms: (of words) formed by adding *~ess*. This used to be quite usual, but many such forms are now thought to be sexist. Words such as *author*, *sculptor*, *poet* are now considered to be neutral terms that should be used to refer to a man or a woman. Some *~ess* words are either still being used or are in a state of flux (*hostess*), while others are unlikely ever to change (*Princess*); *see ~ess*. In general, gender-neutral terms such as *firefighter* are used today, although many of those in popular use (*chair* for *chairperson*, *ms* which is the contraction of *manuscript*) are ambiguous to say the least.

few: the opposite of *many* and meaning *not many*: *few doctors smoke*. When preceded by *a*, it means *a small number of*: *everything depended on a few people*; or *some, but not many*: *I have seen only a few*. It can also mean *a small number, not many*: *many are called but few are chosen*. When preceded by *the* it means the minority or the chosen individuals from a group.

fewer: is apt to be confused with *less* and thus both are often wrongly used. *Fewer* means *a smaller number of* and should be used with plural nouns: *fewer events*, *fewer participants*, *fewer winners*. *Less* means *a smaller amount of* and should be used with singular nouns: *less worry*, *less time*, *less money*; *see* **countable noun**, **uncountable noun**.

figurative: an expressive use of language in which words are used metaphorically not literally, but in a way to suggest resemblances. For example, *mine* in the dictionary sense of *excavation deep into the earth from which minerals are dug* is a literal use of the word. *Mine* in the sense of *he is a mine of information* is a figurative use of the word, implying that the person has a deep reserve of knowledge.

figure of speech: a recognised form of rhetorical expression used to heighten the effect of a statement. The most commonly known are **hyperbole**, **metaphor**, **oxymoron** and **simile** but there are many more, for which individual entries are included.

filled pause: a vocal hesitation (*er, um*).

finger spelling *or* **dactylology:** signing or speaking in which each letter of the alphabet is given its own sign, made with the fingers.

finite verb: a verb that has a tense and has a subject with which it agrees in number and person. For example *smiles* is finite in the sentence *The baby smiles most of the time*. However, in the sentence *I think we should go*, the verb *go* is non-finite since it has no variation of tense and does not have a subject.

finite clause: a clause which contains a finite verb, for example *when he finds them*.

first language: *see* **mother tongue**.

first person: refers to the person who is speaking or writing when referring to himself or herself. The first person pronouns are *I*, *me*, *myself* and *mine*, with the plural forms being *we*, *us*, *ourselves* and *ours*. The first person determiners are *my* and *our*.

fixed phrase *or* **set phrase:** refers to a phrase that has no, or virtually no, variants: *from bad to worse, this and that, rough and ready*.

fluency: the smooth, apparently effortless use of language in speech or writing.

flyting: an exchange of curses or personal abuse in verse form.

focus: an element in a sentence to which the speaker wishes to draw special attention (*It was Peter who drove me there*).

~fold: a suffix meaning *times* or *multiplied by*, as in *a two-fold gain. the share value increased tenfold.*

folk etymology *or* **popular etymology:** the modifying of an unfamilar word or phrase to make it seem to be derived from a more familar word (*sparrowgrass* for *asparagus*).

font *or* **fount:** a complete set of type of a particular design and size.

foot: a group of syllables that form a basic unit of rhythm, especially used in describing poetic metre.

for: a prefix derived from Old English suggesting abstention of some kind (*forgo, forswear* or *forbid*).

fore~: a prefix derived from Old English meaning *beforehand* or *in advance* (*forecast, forewarn*). It can also mean *in front of* (*forecourt*) or *the front part of* (*forehead*) or *preceding* (*forerunner*).

foreign language: a language which is not the mother tongue of a speaker.

foreign plural: nouns borrowed from foreign languages pose a problem in forming the plural. The regular plural ending has been adopted for some: we would naturally say *They sang two more choruses*, not *chori*. Others have retained the original foreign plural (*We seem to have more crises to deal with than ever before* rather than *crisises*) whereas others permit both, as in *I have an entire room full of cactuses / cacti*. People have to learn which form to use when they come across the words for the first time.

Where there is a choice, the classical plural is usually used in the more technical sense (*formulas / formulae, curriculums / curricula*). Just to confuse matters, sometimes the alternative plurals have even developed different senses (*mediums* [scientific or spirits] / *media* [communications] and *appendixes* [bodies and books] / *appendices* [books only]).

foreign expressions: which have been adopted into English, but not naturalised, are sometimes written in italic type (*bête noire* – a fear or obsession; *en passant* – in passing; *en route* – on the way; *bon mot* – a witty saying; *in toto* – completely; and *inter alia* – among other things).

forensic linguistics: the use of linguistic techniques to investigate crimes in which language data constitute part of the evidence.

~form: a suffix meaning *having the form of*, as in *cruciform, cuneiform*, or *having such a number of* as in *uniform, multiform*.

formal: speech or behaviour that is very correct and serious rather than relaxed and friendly, often used in official situations. Something said or written in a formal way has a very ordered, organised method or style; *see also* **informal**.

formant: the characteristic pitch-constituent of a vowel.

form class: a class of linguistic forms with similar or identical grammatical or syntactical features.

formula: a fixed form of words, especially one used in certain social or ceremonial occasions (*Have a nice day, How do you do?, Many happy returns, Yours faithfully, Yours sincerely*).

form word: *see* **function word**.

fortis: said of consonants made with relatively
strong muscular effort and breath force.

fossil: a word that has become obsolete except in
set phrases or forms, e.g. *hue* in *hue and cry*.

fossilised: said of any construction that lacks
productivity, such as idioms (*spick and span*)
and formulaic utterences (*So be it!*).

fragmentary sentence: *see* **major sentence**.

-free: a suffix used to form adjectives indicating
absence of, *free of* / *from* (*carefree*, *lead-free*, *tax-free*).

free form *or* **free morpheme:** a minimal
grammatical unit that can be used as a word
without additional elements.

frequentative: a verb which expresses frequent
repetition or intensity of action. The verb
endings *~le* and *~el* sometimes indicate the
frequentative form (*twinkle*), as can the ending
~er (*chatter*).

fricative *or* **spirant:** said of a consonant made by
the friction of breath in a narrow opening.

-friendly: a modern suffix formed by analogy with
user-friendly to mean *helpful to*, *not-harming*,
supporting, as in *environment-friendly*.

front: said of sounds made in the front part of the
mouth or by the front part (blade) of the tongue.

fronting: in grammar, the moving of a constituent
from the middle or end of a sentence to the front
(*Her hair was golden* / *Golden was her hair*).

~ful: a suffix indicating *the amount that fills
something* (*spoonful*). It can also mean *full of*
(*beautiful*). It can also mean *having the qualities
of* (*masterful*) and *apt to*, *able to* (*forgetful*).

full stop, **point** *or* **period:** a punctuation mark
consisting of a small dot (.). Its principal use is
to end a sentence or to show abbreviation. The
full stop is also used to indicate a decimal point

(*27.5 kilometres*, *9.25 miles*). It can also be used in dates (*18.9.44*), and in showing time (*22.20*).

In modern usage the tendency is to omit full stops from abbreviations. This is most true of abbreviations involving initial capital letters (as in *UNESCO*, *EEC*). Full stops should never be used if one or some of the initial letters do not belong to a full word; thus *electrocardiogram* is abbreviated to *ECG*.

There are usually now no full stops in abbreviations (contractions) formed using the first and last letters of a word (as in *Dr* for doctor and *St* for street), but this is a matter of clarity and taste; some way must be found of distinguishing *Saint* from *street*, for example, where both are prevalent in a piece of writing.

Abbreviations involving the first few letters of a word are the most likely to have full stops, as in *Dec.* (December), but again this is now a matter of taste; for the use of the full stop in direct speech, *see* **direct speech**.

function: the relationship between a linguistic form and the other elements of the system in which it is used, e.g. a noun as subject or object of a clause. It is also used to denote the role language plays in communication, to express ideas, attitudes, or in particular social situations such as the legal or religious.

function change: in grammar, the use of a word in different grammatical roles (*to sit round a table / a round table*).

function word, **form word** or **structure word:** one that has very little meaning but is primarily of grammatical significance, performing a function in a sentence. Function words include determiners, such as *any*, *either* and *the*, and prepositions, such as *in*, *on* and *up*. Words which are not function words are sometimes known as **content words**.

future: a verb form which consists of the auxiliary verb *will* / *shall* / *'ll* followed by the *bare infinitive* of the verb (*I'll leave tomorrow*). It implies that the speaker predicts (assumes) that the event will happen (*It will be Friday tomorrow*), or that the speaker is deciding at the moment of speaking that he or she will do something (*Are you telling me I can't stay here any longer? Well, then, I'll leave tomorrow at dawn*).

There were traditionally clear conventions governing the uses of *shall* and *will*. To express prediction, *shall* was used in the first person (*I* / *We shall go to the seaside tomorrow, weather permitting*), and *will* was to be used with second and third persons (*you* / *he* / *she* / *it* / *they will go into Oxford by bus, it's easier than finding a place to park*). To express intention, *will* was used in the first person, and *shall* with second and third persons: *I will go, and no-one shall stop me, come what may*.

These conventions were promulgated to try to order an area of language which is naturally hazy, and it is now acceptable to use *will* in any situation; the use of *shall* is less common than it used to be, although it persists in both formal language and in some dialect forms.

future continuous: a different way of expressing an action which will be in progress at a future time. It is formed with *will* / *shall* / *'ll* + *be* + *present participle* of the verb (*I'll be leaving tomorrow*). It refers to the progress of the action rather than its result (*You'll be lying on the beach this time next week!*).

future perfect progressive or **future perfect continuous:** composed of the auxiliary *will* / *shall* / *'ll* + *have* + *been* + *present participle* of the verb (*I'll have been married for twelve years in June*). It indicates how long an action or state will have lasted by a certain point in the future.

future perfect simple: composed of the auxiliary *will* / *shall* / *'ll* + *have* + *past participle* of the verb (*I will have finished by eight o'clock*). It indicates that something will have been completed or finished by a certain time in the future.

future time: there are six different ways of expressing future time.

The future, loosely referred to as *future tense*, consists of using the auxiliary verbs *will* / *shall* / *'ll* followed by the *bare infinitive* form of the verb (*I'll leave tomorrow*). It implies a pure prediction — we assume it will happen — or a sudden decision at the moment of speaking.

A common informal way of expressing the future is the use of the form *to be going* followed by the *infinitive* form of the verb (*I'm going to leave*). It implies an intention at the time of speaking, and that the speaker has evidence that the event is going to happen.

The **present progressive**, consisting of the present tense of *to be* followed by the *present participle* (*I'm leaving tomorrow*), implies that the future event has been planned or arranged by somebody.

The **present simple** can be used, as in *I leave tomorrow*, to indicate that the speaker views the event as independent of perception or volition. It is used for schedules (*The train leaves at ten minutes past the hour*).

The more portentous form of the present

G

tense of *to be* followed by the *infinitive* form of
the verb *I am to leave tomorrow*, expresses a fact
imposed by an authority. It is common in
newspapers and in formal writing, for
something that is destined to happen.

The **future progressive**, consisting of *will /
shall / 'll + be + present participle* of the verb (*I'll
be leaving tomorrow*), refers to an action which
will be in progress at a future time. It considers
the progress of the action rather than its result.

The degree of certainty that we attach to a
future event is independent from the verb forms
we use; it can only be expressed by adverbs of
degree, such as *certainly*, *definitely*, *probably*.

~gate: a modern suffix which is added to a noun
denoting something scandalous, whether actual
or alleged, comparable in some way to the
Watergate scandal of 1972. Republican agents
were caught breaking into the headquarters of
the Democratic party in Washington DC, which
were in a building called the Watergate
Building. The uncovering of the attempts to
cover up the break-in led to Richard Nixon's
resignation.

gemination: the doubling of consonants before a
suffix; *see* **doubling of consonants**.

gender: in the English language usually refers to
the natural distinctions of sex, and sexlessness,
that exist, and nouns are classified according to
these distinctions masculine, feminine and
neuter. Masculine nouns include *boy,
bridegroom, brother, cock, drake, duke, emperor,
father, fiancé, fox, heir, hero, husband, king, lion,
man, nephew, prince, son,* and *widower*. Feminine
nouns include *bride, daughter, duchess, duck,*

empress, fiancée, girl, heiress, hen, heroine, lioness, mother, niece, princess, queen, sister, vixen, widow, wife, and *woman*. Neuter nouns include *aeroplane, bicycle, car, carpet, chair, desk, easel, fork, gown, hospital, lamp, table, window*).

Some nouns in English can refer either to a man or a woman, unless the sex is indicated in the context. Such neutral nouns are sometimes said to have **dual gender**. They include *adult, child, cousin, parent, pupil, proprietor, singer, teacher*. Some words in this category were formerly automatically assumed to be masculine and several of them had feminine forms, such as *author / authoress, poet / poetess, sculptor / sculptress*. More recently this has been felt to be sexist, and many of these feminine forms are now rarely used. However others, such as *actress* and *waitress*, are still in common use; *see* ~**ess**.

In many languages grammatical gender plays a major part. In French, for example, all nouns are either masculine or feminine although there are also many feminine forms of masculine nouns such as *la pharmacienne / le pharmacien*. There is no neuter classification at all. In German, as in English, there are three grammatical genders: masculine, feminine and neuter; in addition there are feminine forms of masculine nouns such as *die Apothekerin / der Apotheker*, although in each case the English translation would be *chemist*. However, grammatical gender in English is not relevant except in the third personal singular pronouns, *he / him / his / himself, she / her / hers / herself* and *it / it / its / itself*. Traditionally, the masculine form was considered an acceptable pronoun not just for nouns of the masculine gender, but also for those of neutral or dual gender as well: *Each parent must be responsible for his own child*. In order to avoid this, some people use *he or she*, *his or her*, as in *Each parent must be responsible for his or her own child*. The other common solution is to be ungrammatical and use a plural pronoun: *Each parent must be responsible for their own child*. It is usually possible to avoid being both sexist and ungrammatical by rephrasing: *All parents must be responsible for their own children*.

generic: a word or sentence characteristic of or relating to a class: *the Japanese*.

genitive case: indicates possession or ownership. It is usually marked by an *s* and an apostrophe (as in *'s* or *s'*). Many spelling errors centre on the position of the *s* in relation to the apostrophe. Nouns in the genitive case are usually formed by adding *'s* to the singular noun (*the dog's collar*); by adding an apostrophe to plural nouns that end in ~*s* (*all the dogs' collars*); by adding *'s* to irregular plural nouns that do not end in ~*s* (*women's shoes*). In the genitive form of a name or singular noun which ends in ~*s*, ~*x* or ~*z*, the apostrophe may or may not be followed by *s*. The final *s* is almost always added (*James's book*) for words of one syllable.

The final *s* is most frequently omitted in names, particularly in names of three or more syllables (*Euripides' plays*). In many cases the presence or absence of a final *s* is a matter of convention. Apostrophes are often wrongly omitted in modern usage, particularly in the media and by advertisers (*girls jeans*). Conversely, apostrophes are almost as often erroneously added (*potato's 50p a kilo*) because of uncertainty as to when not to use the apostrophe.

A group genitive occurs when more than one noun is involved, with only one *'s* being used, as in *Bourne and Hollingsworth's former site*.

The alternative genitive construction involves the use of *of* (*the pages of the book*). In general, proper nouns and animate beings tend to take the *'s* ending and inanimate objects tend to take the *of* construction.

genre: an identifiable kind or style, especially of art or literature: *still-life painting*, *the detective novel*, *drawing-room comedy*, *kitchen-sink drama*.

geo~: a prefix derived from Greek and indicating *earth* (*geography*, *geochemistry*, *geocentric*).

geographical features: their names should be written with initial capital letters. These include the common nouns that are part of the name of the feature: *Great Victoria Desert*, *Sturt Creek*, *Lake Moore*, *Kimberley Plateau*, *Coral Sea*, *Bass Strait*, *Snowy Mountains*.

geographical linguistics, **areal linguistics** *or* **linguistic geography:** the study of languages and dialects in terms of their regional distribution.

gerund: the *~ing* form of a verb when it functions as a noun, sometimes referred to as a verbal noun. It has the same form as the present participle, but has a different function. For example, in the sentence *He was running round the track*, the word *running* is the present participle in the verb phrase *was running*, but in the sentence *Reading is his idea of relaxation*, the word *reading* is a gerund because it acts as a noun as the subject of the sentence.

get: sometimes used to form the passive voice instead of the verb *to be*. The use of the verb *to get* to form the passive (*They get their new car* *tomorrow*; *We got our new car today*), is sometimes considered to be more informal than the use of *be*. Often there is more action involved when the *get* construction is used than when *be* is used, since *get* is a more dynamic verb.

Get, as a verb in the active form, is frequently overused. Such overuse should be avoided, particularly in formal contexts. The word can often be replaced by a synonym such as *obtain*, *acquire* or *receive*. Thus, *If you are getting a new car, perhaps you should get a bank loan* could be rephrased as *If you want to acquire a new car, perhaps you could obtain a bank loan*.

Got, the past tense of *get*, is often used unnecessarily (*We have got enough food to last us the week*); here *have* is sufficient on its own.

ghost form: a word that originates from an error made during the transcribing, copying, analysing, or learning of a language, which does not exist in the original language.

given information: *see* **topic**.

glide: a transitional sound made as the vocal organs move towards (on-glide) or away from (off-glide) an articulation.

gliding vowel: *see* **diphthong**.

glossary: an alphabetical list of terms or words found in or relating to a specific subject or text.

glottal: sounds made in the larynx by closing or narrowing the glottis, for example a whisper.

glottalisation: an articulation involving a simultaneous glottal constriction.

glottal stop: a sound produced by the sudden opening or shutting of the glottis.

glottis: the aperture at the upper end of the windpipe and between the vocal folds.

goal: can be used to describe the recipient or

object of the action of a verb, the opposite of agent or actor. Thus, in the sentence *The dog chased the cat*, the noun *dog* is the agent or actor and *cat* is the goal.

gobbledygook: used informally to refer to pompous or unintelligible **jargon**.

govern: said about a verb or preposition in relation to a noun or pronoun; it indicates that the verb or preposition has a dependant noun or pronoun. Thus, in the phrase *by the door*, the preposition *by* is said to govern the noun *door*.

gradable: said of adjectives and adverbs to denote that they can take degrees of comparison. Thus *warm* is a gradable adjective since it has a comparative form (*warmer*) and a superlative form (*warmest*). Such words as *supreme* and *unique*, which cannot normally have a comparative or superlative form, are termed **non-gradable**.

~gram: a suffix derived from Greek and denoting a thing written or recorded, often in a special way (*anagram, diagram, epigram, monogram, telegram*). It is also used in modern usage to indicate a *greeting* or *message* (*kissogram*).

grammar: the branch of language study or linguistics which deals with the means of showing the relation between words as used in speech or writing, traditionally divided into the study of inflections (or morphology) and the structure of sentences (syntax), and often also including phonology.

grammatical: said of constructions that conform to the rules of a grammar.

~graph: a suffix derived from Greek and indicating that something is written or drawn in a specific way (*autograph, photograph*). It is also used to indicate an instrument that records in written form (*heliograph, seismograph, tachograph*).

grapheme: the smallest meaningful segment in a piece of writing or print.

graphetics: the study of the visual properties of written or printed language.

graphology: the study of handwriting as a guide to discover the writer's character.

grave accent: *see* **accent**.

groove: a type of fricative consonant produced when the tongue is slightly hollowed along its central line.

group noun: *see* **collective noun**

gynaeco~: a prefix derived from Greek and indicating *female, woman* or *women*, as in *gynaecocracy, gynaecology, gynaecomastia*.

habitual: refers to the action, especially of a verb or an adverb, that occurs regularly and repeatedly. The *habitual present* is found in such sentences as *He walks the dog at six every night.* This is in contrast to the *stative present*, which indicates the action of the verb that occurs at all times (*Children grow up*). There is also a *habitual past* tense: *He worked night and day for the money to buy that car; see also* **tense**.

haemo~: a prefix derived from Greek and meaning *blood*, as in *haemoglobin, haemophilia*.

haiku: a short Japanese three-part poem, usually of 17 syllables in lines of 5-7-5 syllables. The traditional subject matter is usually images of the natural world. A master of the form was the Japanese samurai Matsuo Munefusa (1644–94), who wrote poetry as Matsuo Basho:

On | a | with|ered| branch
A | cr|ow| has | a|light|ed
Night | fall | in | au|tumn.

half *and* **halve:** are liable to be confused. *Half* is a noun, an adjective, an adverb, a quantifier or a pronoun, and *halve* is the verb. *Half* is followed by a singular noun when it is referring to an amount: *Half of the loaf has been eaten*. It is followed by a plural verb when it is referring to a number: *Half of the cakes have been eaten*, *Half of the delegates have already left the conference*.

The plural of *half* is *halves*: *They served halves of melon with port*, and it is apt to be confused with the verb *to halve*. *She halved the sweets between the two children* is an example of the verb *to halve*, as is *He halved his estate's liability to inheritance tax by transferring ownership of his house to his grandchildren*.

~hand: a suffix meaning *worker*, as in *deckhand*, *farmhand* and *short-handed*. It can also mean *position*, as in *right-hand* and *left-hand*.

hanged *and* **hung:** both are past tenses and past participles of the verb *to hang* but they are not interchangeable. *Hanged* is restricted to the meaning *suspended by the neck until dead*, as in *He was hanged for the murder of six people*. However, *hung* is the more general form, as in *The pictures were hung in the gallery in London*.

hanging participle: *see* **dangling participle**.

have: a verb which has several functions. One major use is as an auxiliary verb in forming the perfect tense and past perfect tense, or pluperfect tense, of other verbs' tenses. It helps to form these tenses in conjunction with the past participle of the verb in question.

The perfect tense of a verb is formed by the present tense of the verb *to have* and the *past participle* of the verb. Examples include *They have won the Cup*; *The team has lost*; *The ref has fallen over*; *They have grabbed the lead*; *We have entered the final few minutes*.

The past perfect or pluperfect is formed by the past tense of the verb *have* and the *past participle* of the verb in question: *She had asked the teacher to repeat the question*; *They had not understood the question*; *The girl had kept quiet*; *His mother had taken him to school*; *The headmaster had spoken to all of the pupils*; *They had rushed out when the bell rang*.

Both perfect tenses and past perfect or pluperfect tenses are often contracted in speech or in informal written English: *We've had enough to eat*; *You've ruined my dress*; *He's missed the bus*; *They'd left too late*; *She'd wanted a new pair of shoes*; *He'd picked the wrong horse*.

Have is also used as a verb on its own in the sense of *possess* or *own*: *We have enough food to feed them all if the whole family turns up*. In spoken or in informal English, *have got* is often used, as in *We've got enough food if they do turn up*. This use should be avoided, certainly in formal English, because *got* is superfluous.

It is also used to indicate suffering from an illness or disease, as in *I have a bad back*; *he has a severe case of jaundice*; *the whole family has flu*.

In the expression *have to*, *have* is often used to mean that something must be done. In the present tense *have to* can be used instead of *must*: *I have to go now*. If the *something that must be done* refers to the future, the future form *will have to* is used: *I will have to go to the shops later*. If the *something that must be done* refers to the past, *had to* is used: *I had to go to the shops yesterday*.

It may also be used to indicate that an activity is taking place, in the sense of *being caused to happen*: *We're having a new kitchen fitted*; *we had the house re-wired last year*; *he will have it re-thatched rather than tiled*.

he: a personal pronoun that is used as the subject of a sentence or clause to refer to a man, boy, or male animal. It is thus said to be a *masculine* personal pronoun. Since *he* refers to a third party and does not refer to the speaker or the person being addressed, it is a *third-person pronoun*: *Eric is very happy, he has passed the exam*.

He traditionally was used to refer not only to nouns relating to the masculine sex but also to nouns that are now regarded as being neutral or of **dual gender**, including *artist, author, doctor, dentist, teacher, pupil*. Without further information it is impossible to know to which sex such nouns are referring. It used to be considered acceptable to write or say *I need to find a new dentist but every time I have a recommendation to follow up, he is too busy to see me*, whether or not the writer or speaker knew that the dentist in question was a man. In current usage it is regarded as sexist to imply that the person is masculine by using *he* to refer to any of them, unless the context clearly indicates that the noun in question refers to a man or boy.

It is possible to use the convention *he or she*: *Every artist knows that he or she can expect to endure many years of hardship*. However this does sound clumsy, particularly in spoken or informally written English. Many people prefer to be ungrammatical and use the plural personal pronoun *they* instead of *he or she* in certain situations, as in *Every artist knows that they can expect to endure many years of hardship*. However, it is usually possible to rephrase the sentence in order to achieve agreement between the noun and the pronoun: *All artists know that they can expect to endure many years of hardship*.

head: the main element controlling the function of a phrase, on which the other elements depend.

~head: *see* **~hood**.

headline: the heading at the top of an article or page, especially in a newspaper. By their nature, headlines must generally be quite brief, partly because of shortage of space and partly to capture the attention of the potential reader. Definite and indefinite articles and other minor words tend to be omitted in order to achieve this; the future tense may be represented by a to-infinitive (*President to quit*), and present tenses are often misused for past events. Whether intentionally or not, sometimes the effect may be salacious or comical; *Councillors lash galloping girls* headed an article concerning the alleged misuse of grass verges by horseriders.

This shorthand form of headline language has coined such usage as *tug-of-love baby* to describe a child whose custody is being bitterly fought over, which originated as headline terms but now are quite common in the general language.

heading: a title at the head of a page, section of a book or other printed document. These are often written using initial capital letters, except for articles or prepositions (*The Inner World of Childhood*), but this is a matter of taste or of house style. Some people prefer to use lower-case letters except for the first word (*The inner world of childhood*), others to use only capital letters (THE INNER WORLD OF CHILDHOOD). Headings may be underlined, italicised, or emboldened for emphasis.

headword *or* **entry word:** a word which is at the
head of an entry in a dictionary or encyclopedia.
It is usually written in bold type so that it
stands out on the page and is readily identifiable.

helping verb: see **auxiliary verb**.

hemi~: a prefix derived from Greek and meaning
half, as in *hemicycle, hemispherical, hemizygous.*

hendiadys: a figure of speech in which an idea is
expressed by two words connected by *and*,
instead of one modifying the other (*safe and
sound* instead of *safely sound*).

he / she: *see* **he.**

her: the third-person feminine singular personal
pronoun. It acts as the object in a sentence:
Have you seen her recently?; *see* **he.**

hers: the third person feminine singular personal
pronoun. It in the possessive case: *Are you sure
that this house is hers?*; *see* **his**; **her** and **possessive**.

hetero~: a prefix derived from Greek and meaning
other or *different*, as in *heterodox, heterodyne,
heterogeneous, heteronym, heterosexual.*

hexa~: a prefix derived from Greek and meaning
six, as in *hexachord, hexadecimal, hexagon.*

hexameter: a line of verse of six metrical feet.

hiatus: a break between two vowels coming
together in different syllables, as in *co-operate*
and *Goyaesque.*

hierarchy: a classification of linguistic units into
a series of successively subordinate levels,
especially an analysis of sentences into clauses,
phrases, words and morphemes.

high: vowels, and occasionally consonants, that
are sounded by raising the tongue towards the
roof of the mouth.

him: the third person masculine singular personal
pronoun when used as the object of a sentence

or clause, as in *She was unable to find him*. *Him* traditionally was used to apply not only to masculine nouns such as *man* and *boy*, but also to nouns that are said to be of **dual gender**. These include *artist*, *author*, *child*, *parent*, *pupil* and *teacher*.

When there is no further information from the context, it is not possible for the listener or reader to know the sex of the person referred to by any of these words. Whereas formerly it was acceptable to write or say *The child must take a clean handkerchief with him*, in current usage this is considered sexist and there is a modern convention that *him / her* should be used instead, as in *The child must take a clean handkerchief with him / her*. This convention is felt by some people to be cumbersome, particularly in spoken and in informal English, and so the ungrammatical use of the plural personal pronoun *them* instead has become widespread. *The child must take a clean handkerchief with them* is a particularly unacceptable example of this usage because it raises doubt as to the number of children involved, and here it would certainly be better to rephrase the sentence: *All children must take a clean handkerchief with them*; *see* ~**ess**, **he**.

him *or* **her:** *see* **him**.

his: the third personal singular masculine pronoun when used to indicate possession: *He was hiding from his sister*. Traditionally *his* was used to refer not only to masculine nouns, such as *man*, *boy*, and so on, but also to what are known as nouns of **dual gender**. These include *artist*, *author*, *child*, *parent*, *pupil* and *teacher*. Without further information from the context it is not possible for the listener or the reader to know the sex of the person referred to by one of these words. Formerly it was considered acceptable to use *his* in such situations, as in *Each of the teachers is responsible for his pupils' behaviour*. Currently this is considered sexist, and there is a modern convention that *his or her* should be used instead to circumvent allegations of bias, as in *Each of the teachers is responsible for his or her pupils' behaviour*. This convention in turn is patently clumsy, and some people prefer to use the ungrammatical plural personal pronoun *their*, as in *Each of the teachers is responsible for their pupils' behaviour*. Since both teachers and pupils are plural, the likelihood is that both groups include both genders, so it is preferable to recast the sentence in a gender-neutral form: *All of the teachers are responsible for their pupils behaviour*; see ~**ess**, **he**, **him**.

his *or* her: *see* **his**.

historical linguistics, comparative philology *or* **diachronic linguistics:** the study of the development of language and languages over time.

historical present: the use of a present tense form while narrating events which happened in the past: *I was just walking along minding my own business when I see an armed robbery at the bank*.

holidays: in the sense of public holidays or festivals, should be written with an initial capital letter, as in *Christmas Day*.

holograph: a document wholly written in the handwriting of the person named as the author.

holophrase: a grammatically unstructured utterance, usually consisting of a single word, typical of the first words spoken by a baby, as in *Dada*.

homo~: a prefix derived from Greek and meaning *same*, as in *homodyne*, *homoeopathy*, *homologous*.

homograph: words that have the same spellings but different pronunciations, meanings or origins. Homographs include:

bow, a verb, pronounced to rhyme with *how*, meaning to bend the head or body as a sign of respect or in greeting; *bow*, a noun, pronounced to rhyme with *low*, meaning a looped knot, tied in a string or ribbon.

lead, a verb, pronounced *leed*, meaning to show the way; *lead*, a noun, pronounced *led*, meaning a type of heavy greyish metal used for roofing.

row, a noun, pronounced to rhyme with *low*, meaning a number of people or things arranged in a line; *row*, another noun, pronounced to rhyme with *how*, meaning a quarrel or a disagreement.

sow, a verb, pronounced to rhyme with *low*, meaning to scatter seeds in the earth; *sow*, a noun, pronounced to rhyme with *how*, meaning a female pig.

wind, a noun, pronounced to rhyme with *sinned*, meaning a force of air; *wind*, a verb, pronounced to rhyme with *shined*, meaning to meander.

homonym: refers to a word having the same sound or the same spelling as another, but a different meaning and origin. Examples include:

bill, a noun, meaning a written statement of money owed or a written or printed advertisement; *bill*, a noun, meaning a bird's beak.

fair, an adjective, meaning variously attractive, equitable, free from prejudice, light in colour, or pleasant weather; *fair*, a noun, originally meaning a market held regularly in the same place, but now simply applied to an event with entertainments and rides or one for a particular trade, allowing commercial concerns to exhibit their wares and promote their services.

pulse, a noun, meaning the throbbing caused by the contractions of the heart; *pulse*, a noun, meaning the edible seeds of any of various crops of the pea family, such as lentils, peas and beans.

row, a verb, meaning to propel a boat by means of the action of the oars on the water; *row*, a noun, meaning a number of people or things arranged in a line.

homophone: two or more words which sound the same but have different meanings, origins, or spellings; for examples, *see* **Appendix**, *page 211*.

~hood *or* **~head:** a suffix meaning *condition*, *group* or *state*, as in *brotherhood, falsehood, neighbourhood, sisterhood*; *breadhead, nethead, stresshead*.

hybrid: a word that is composed from words or elements derived from different languages, as in *television* which is taken from Greek and Latin.

hydro~: a prefix derived from Greek and, generally, meaning *water* (*hydrofoil*). It can also mean *hydrogen*, however, as in *hydrochloride*.

hydronymy: the study of the names of rivers, lakes, and other bodies of water.

hyper~: a prefix derived from Greek meaning *above, beyond, exceeding, over*, or *excessively* (*hyperactive, hypercritical, hyperinflation, hyperphysical, hypersensitive, hypersonic*).

hyperbole: a figure of speech consisting of exaggeration or over-statement, used for emphasis, and not meant to be taken literally (*I could eat a horse; there were millions of people in the park; the wretched brat, I could have killed him*).

hypercorrection, **hyperurbanism** *or* **over-correction:** a linguistic form that goes beyond what is necessary, because of the speaker's desire to be correct (*up with which I will not put*).

hypo~: a prefix derived from Greek and meaning *under*, as in *hypothermia*, *hypodermic*.

hyphen: a small stroke (-) used to join two words semantically or syntactically, or to show the division of a word at the end of a line, or to indicate a missing or implied element. It is used:

- before abbreviations (*pro-UN*, *anti-NATO*).
- before dates or numbers (*pre-1066*, *post-2000*).
- for clarity: for example, in *Can you re-cover my sofa?*, *re-cover* is spelt with a hyphen in order to differentiate it from *to recover*, meaning to get better after an illness. Similarly, to avoid ambiguity, *re-form*, meaning *to form again*, is written with a hyphen to differentiate it from *reform*, meaning *to improve*.
- to join words formed with the prefix *ex-*, as in *ex-wife*.
- to join words formed with the prefix *non-*, as in *non-functional*. The hyphen may be omitted, but at present both forms are common.
- to join words formed with the prefix *self-*, as in *self-important*.
- to join a prefix to a proper noun (*anti-Semitic*, *post-Victorian*, *pre-Christmas*, *pro-vicechancellor*).
- to separate a prefix from the main element of a word which begins with a vowel, as in *pre-ordain*. Despite the growing tendency to omit the hyphen in such cases, if the omission of the hyphen results in double *i*, the hyphen should always be retained (*semi-independent*).
- in fixed compounds of two or three or more words, as in *mother-in-law*.

- in compound adjectives consisting of two elements, the second of which ends in ~*ed*, hyphens are usually used (*fair-haired*).
- in compound adjectives used before nouns, hyphens are usually used (*gas-fired central heating*).
- in compounds containing some adverbs, hyphens are usually used to avoid ambiguity (*his best-known work*). Generally an adverb ending in ~*ly* before adjectives and participles is not hyphenated (*a highly respected artist*).
- in compounds newly formed from phrasal verbs, generally hyphens are used, but tend to be omitted as the expression passes into common usage. Thus both *take-over / takeover*, *run-down / rundown* are common. However, there are some words formed from phrasal verbs that are usually spelt without a hyphen, as in *breakthrough*.
- in compound numerals from 21 to 99 when they are written out in full (*sixty-nine years ago*). Compound numbers (*six hundred*) are not otherwise hyphenated, but hyphens are used in fractions (*three-quarters*), and in number phrases (*a twelfth-century monastery*).
- to break words at the ends of lines. People used to be more careful about where they broke words, doing so according to etymological principles, but there is a growing tendency to break words according to the way in which they are pronounced. Some dictionaries or spelling dictionaries give help with the division and hyphenation of individual words. General points are that one-syllable words should not be divided and words should not be broken after the first letter of a word or

immediately before the last letter. Care
should be taken not to break up words in such
a way as to mislead the reader, for example by
forming elements that are words in their own
right, such as *mans-laughter* should be avoided.
It is particularly important to check any
writing for this type of error which has been
prepared by means of computer software, as
these are generally programmed to break
between two consonants. Proper nouns should
not be broken, unless they fall naturally into
two or more parts; *Eng-land* is not acceptable,
but it would be permissible to break John / Doe.

- when two or more compound hyphenated
adjectives with the same second element
qualify the same noun, the common element
need not be repeated but grammatically the
hyphen should be (*one-* or *two-bedroomed flats*).
Many typographers strongly oppose the practice.

The use or non-use of the hyphen is often a
matter of choice, house style or frequency of
usage. Currently there is a tendency to use any
punctuation marks less frequently than was
formerly the practice, and so today the use of
the hyphen (as in *dining-room* / *dining room*), is
less frequent. The length of compound nouns
often affects the inclusion or omission of the
hyphen. Compounds of two short elements that
are well-established words tend not to be
hyphenated (*bedroom*, *whitewash*), whereas
compound words with more syllables are more
likely to be hyphenated (*bottle-washer*).

hyperurbanism: *see* **hypercorrection**.

hypocoristic: a pet name (*sweetheart*, *Mike*, *Sue*).

hypostatise: to speak of an abstract quality as if it
were human.

I and **me**: the first person singular pronoun, but *I* acts as the subject of a sentence and *me* as the object. In answer to such questions as *Who is there?* the grammatically correct reply is *It is I.* However, *It is me* is widespread except in the most formal contexts, especially when spoken, and should not be assumed to be less polite than *I*.

Confusion does arise as to whether to use *I* or *me* after *between*. Since *between* is followed by an object, *me* is the correct form. Thus it is correct to say *Just between you and me.* On the other hand, *I*, being a subject, should be used in such sentences as *You and I have both played for the county. Me* should be reserved for such sentences as *They asked you and me to edit the whole series*, since in this case it is the object form of the first person singular that is required. In such sentences it is often helpful mentally to eliminate the first object of the pair as a test — *They asked I to edit the whole series* is clearly wrong.

iamb *or* **iambus**: a unit of metre consisting of a short (unstressed) syllable followed by a long (stressed) syllable (*see-saw*).

~ian: a suffix indicating either a *profession*, *job* or *pastime* (*librarian*, *electrician*, *musician*), or an adjective formed from a proper name (*Edwardian*).

~iana: a suffix indicating memorabilia (*Victoriana*).

~ible: *see* **adjective**.

iconic: said of signals which embody a characteristic of the thing they signify, such as **onomatopœia**.

~ics: a suffix indicating *arts*, *science*, or *action* (as in *ethics*, *phonetics*, *genetics*, *physics*, *athletics*).

ictus: rhythmical or metrical stress.

identifying relative clause: *see* **defining relative clause**.

ideogram: a written character that symbolises a

concept without indicating the pronunciation, such as £, &, +.

idiolect: to the speech habits, knowledge and command of language of an individual.

idiom: a phrase, established by usage, the meaning of which cannot be easily deduced from the individual meanings of the words it contains:

to know the ropes, a nautical idiom. In the days of sailing ships, if a sailor was being taught the basic techniques of seamanship he would have had to be taught the mechanics of ropes, which were of prime importance because they controlled the sails. Hence *to know the ropes* has come to mean *to understand the procedures and details involved in something; how it functions.*

out on a limb means *in a risky and perhaps lonely position*, this being a reference to someone being stuck in an isolated and precarious position on the branch of a tree. Literally it refers to a person or animal that has crawled so far out on a branch of a tree that he / she is in danger of falling or of not being able to crawl back to the main tree.

to throw someone to the lions means *deliberately to put someone in a difficult or dangerous position.* In order fully to appreciate the meaning of the idiom, the reader or listener has to understand that it refers to a practice in ancient Rome, supposedly a form of entertainment, in which prisoners of war or conscience were thrown to hungry wild animals in an arena, to be attacked and killed.

to throw in the towel means *to give in, to admit defeat.* This idiom comes from the world of boxing, in which *throwing in the towel* indicates a method of conceding defeat.

to sell someone down the river means *to betray or be disloyal to someone*. The origin of this expression is American, as it refers to slave owners in the Mississippi states of the United States, who sold their slaves to buyers downstream in Louisiana where living and working conditions were much harder.

Such idioms as *to sell someone down the river* are known as opaque idioms since there is no evident connection between the meaning of the individual words of the idiom and the idiom itself. Idioms such as *to keep a straight face* are known as transparent idioms since, although they are not to be interpreted literally, it is reasonably obvious what they mean.

The following idiomatic expressions were all introduced to us by Shakespeare, and now form part of our modern language:

all our yesterdays (Macbeth)
as good luck would have it (The Merry Wives of Windsor).
beggars all description (Antony and Cleopatra)
a foregone conclusion (Othello)
hoist on his own petard (Hamlet)
love is blind (Merchant of Venice)
to the manner born (Hamlet)
in my mind's eye (Hamlet)
at one fell swoop (Macbeth)
I must be cruel to be kind (Hamlet)
a tower of strength (Richard III)
with bated breath (Merchant of Venice)
what the dickens (The Merry Wives of Windsor)

i.e.: the abbreviation of the Latin phrase *id est*, meaning *that is to say*. It is used before explanations or amplifications of what has just been mentioned (*As from tomorrow you're grounded,* *i.e. not allowed out after school*). It is usually spelt with a full stop after each of the letters.

if: a conjunction which is often used to introduce an **adverbial subordinate clause of condition** (*If I had realised that it was going to rain I should have taken an umbrella*). *If* may also introduce a **subordinate clause** (*He asked if we had seen it*).

~ify: a suffix indicating *making* or *becoming* (*signify*, *simplify*, *solidify*).

imagery: the use of metaphor, simile, and other figurative language, especially as used by an author for particular effects.

imperative: the verb mood that expresses commands. The verbs in the following phrases are in the imperative mood: *Come here! Go away! Leave that alone! Answer me! Sit down!* All of these examples with verbs in the imperative mood sound rather imperious or dictatorial and end with an exclamation mark, but not all expressions with verbs in the imperative mood require the use of the exclamation mark. These sentences also have verbs in the imperative mood: *Have another piece of cake*; *Turn left at the lights*. Sentences with verbs in the imperative mood are known as imperative sentences.

imperfect: any tense that denotes an action in progress, not fully formed or done, incomplete at the time in question. The term derives from the classification in Latin grammar and was traditionally applied to the past imperfect (*They were standing there*).

The imperfect has now been largely superseded by the **progressive / continuous tense**, which is marked by the use of *be + present participle* of the verb. Continuous tenses are used when talking about temporary situations at a particular point in time (*They were waiting for a train*).

impersonal: a verb which is used only with a formal subject, usually *it*, and expressing an action not attributable to a definite subject (*It is snowing*).

inclusive: said of a first person pronoun that refers to both the speaker and someone else, e.g. when *we* means *me and you*. The term is used also of deliberately non-sexist language, especially that avoiding the use of masculine pronouns to mean women as well as men.

indefinite article: the word (*a* and *an* in English) preceding a noun but implying no particular example of that noun; *see* **a**, **an**.

indefinite pronoun: refers to people or things without being specific as to exactly who or what they are. The class includes *anyone*, *everything*, *somebody*.

indention: a line of writing or print that begins further in from the margins than the rest of the passage. In most text, the first line of a paragraph is indented; in this dictionary, the second and subsequent lines of each entry are indented, in order to give more prominence to the headwords.

independent clause: refers to a clause which makes sense without being dependent on another clause (as in *The car has two doors*). **Main clauses**, also known as **principal clauses**, are independent clauses and in the sentence *I'll remember to telephone when I get home*, the clause *I'll remember to telephone* is an independent clause, and *when I get home* is a dependent clause.

indexical: those features of speech or writing (especially voice quality) that reveal the personal characteristics of the owner, such as age or sex.

indicative: the mood of a verb which makes a simple statement of fact (*He was waiting for the bus*). It is known also as the declarative mood; the others are the **imperative** and the **subjunctive**.

indirect object: an object which is used with a transitive verb to indicate who benefits from an action or gets something as a result. Usually, if there is an indirect object, there is also a direct object.

The prepositions *to* and *for* precede the indirect object if it follows the direct object, as in *I took it to the policeman on duty*, where *it* is the direct object, and *to the policeman on duty* is the indirect object. If the indirect object comes before the direct object, there is no preposition introducing it (*I'll lend you some*), where *some* is the direct object and *you* is the indirect object.

An indirect object can be a noun, and in the sentence *I sent our neighbour a card*, *our neighbour* is an indirect object. In the sentence *Mum bought this ice-cream for Anne*, *for Anne* is the indirect object.

An indirect object can be a noun phrase, and in the sentence *She sent some flowers to the nurse in charge of her daughter's hospital ward*, *to the nurse in charge of her daughter's hospital ward* is the indirect object.

An indirect object can be a pronoun, and in the sentence *Give it (to) me*, *(to) me* is the indirect object. In the sentence *Could you do that for us?*, *for us* is the indirect object.

Some of the verbs that are used with an indirect object are *to bring, to buy, to cost, to give, to leave, to lend, to make, to offer, to owe, to pass, to pay, to promise, to read, to refuse, to send, to show, to take, to tell, to write.*

The verbs *to explain* and *to suggest* must be used with a preposition before an indirect object; *see* **object**, **direct object**.

indirect question: appears in reported speech, as in *We asked them what they were going to see.*

indirect speech *or* **reported speech:** a way of reporting what someone has said without using the actual words used by the speaker. There is usually an introductory verb and a subordinate clause introduced by *that*, as in *He said that he was resigning today.* In **direct speech** this sentence would become *He said, 'I am resigning today'.* When the change is made from direct speech to indirect speech, the pronouns, adverbs of time and place, and tenses are changed to accord with the viewpoint of the person doing the reporting.

infinitive: the base form of a verb, expressing the verbal notion without any indication of person, number or tense. There are two forms of the infinitive. One is the to-infinitive form, *They decided to leave.*

The other form of the infinitive is called the bare infinitive. This form consists of the base form of the verb only, without *to*, as in *We saw him leave*; *see* **split infinitive**.

inflect: to change the form of a word by means of an **affix** in order to express the case, number, gender, or mood. Nouns inflect for possession (*boy's, children's, girl's, parents', pupil's, teacher's*) and plural (*aeroplanes, buildings, cats, cows, pigs, pumpkins, tables, trains*); some adjectives inflect for the comparative form (*handsomer, higher, wider*); verbs inflect for the third person singular of the indicative present (*I bounce / it bounces*, *I catch / she catches*, *I throw / he throws*), also inflect for the present participle (*bouncing*, *catching*, *throwing*), and for the past participle (*bounced*, *caught*, *threw*). In phonetics, to inflect is to change the pitch of the voice; for example, a rising inflection for a question.

inflection: the act or condition of inflecting or being inflected. It also refers to an inflected form of a word or a suffix or other element used to inflect a word, such as *~ed*; *see* **inflect**.

informal: style of language, often spoken, that has a simpler grammatical structure and simpler vocabulary, often colloquial or even slangy.

infra~: a prefix derived from Latin and indicating *below* or *beneath* (*infrasonic*, *infrastructure*) or within (*infraposed*, *infraspecific*).

~ing: a suffix to verb roots, which may be either present participles or **gerunds**. **Present participles** are used in the formation of the progressive or continuous tenses, as in *We were looking in the window*. Present participles can also be used in non-finite clauses or phrases, as in *Walking along, she considered what she should do*.

Gerunds act as nouns and are sometimes known as *verbal nouns* (*Smoking is bad for one's health*).

A large number of adjectives end in *~ing*. Many of these have the same form as the present participle of a transitive verb and are similar in meaning, for example *an interesting idea*. Some *~ing* adjectives are related to intransitive verbs, for example *increasing responsibilities*. Some *~ing* adjectives are related to the forms of verbs but have different meanings from the verbs, such as in *an engaging personality*. Other *~ing* adjectives are not related to verbs at all, for example *appetising*, *enterprising*, *impending*. Some ~*ing* adjectives are used informally for emphasis: *a blinding flash of inspiration*, *a racking cough*, *a stinking headache*, *a wrenching farewell*.

~**ingly:** a suffix forming adverbs especially denoting manner of action, nature or condition (*charmingly*, *lovingly*, *slightingly*).

initialism: usage of words made up from initial letters, each letter being pronounced separately (*BBC*, *VIP*); a common habit in bureaucratic circles and in the armed services in particular.

intensifier: refers to a word or prefix used to give force or emphasis: *scarcely*, *thoroughly*, *totally*.

inter~: a prefix of Latin origin and indicating *between* or *among*, as in *intercontinental*.

interdental: a consonant pronounced by the tip of the tongue between the teeth.

interjections: an exclamation, especially as part of a speech. Sometimes they are formed by actual words and sometimes they simply consist of sounds indicating emotion: *ah!*, *oh!*, *gosh!*, *phew!*, *ouch!*, *tut-tut!*, *alas!*, *dear me!*.

internal rhyme: the rhyming of words within lines of verse, rather than only at the ends of the lines.

International Phonetic Alphabet (IPA): a system of written symbols designed to enable the speech sounds of any language to be consistently represented. It is based on the Roman and Greek alphabets, with the addition of some special symbols and diacritical marks. The alphabet was first published in 1889.

interrogative adjective *or* **determiner:** an adjective or determiner that asks a question in relation to the nouns which they qualify (*What kind of book do you like best?*; *Which book did you read* *first over the holiday?*; *Whose dog-eared book is this?*; *Whose dog attacked the postman yesterday?*).

interrogative adverb: an adverb that asks a question (*How was that long train journey?*; *When will the ferry depart for the island?*; *Where does this bus go to?*; *Why was the bus so late last night?*).

interrogative pronoun: a pronoun that asks a question (*Who knows the answer?*; *What is the question?*; *Whose are these answers?*; *To whom did you address the question?*).

interrogative sentence: a sentence that asks a question (*Who is going?*; *Where is he going?*; *Why have they gone?*; *What did they go for?*; *Which do you prefer?*). Sentences which take the form of a question do not always seek information, or expect a reply. Sometimes they are exclamations (*Can you believe it? Did you ever see anything like it?*). Some interrogative sentences are known as rhetorical questions, which are asked purely for effect and require no answer (*Where will it all end?*).

Sentences which take the form of questions may function as statements (*Isn't that always the case?*) or may really be commands or directives (*Could you turn the light on? Would you like to do your homework now?*).

intervocalic: a consonant used between two vowels.

intonation: the modulation of the voice, the use of changes of pitch or monotone.

intra~: a prefix of Latin origin and indicating *on the inside* or *within* (*intracellular, intramural, intranational, intranet, intravascular*).

intransitive verb: a verb which neither takes nor requires a direct object (*I wonder why*; *You always argue*; *My instructors despair*; *We all die*).

Many verbs can be either transitive or intransitive, according to the context. Thus *played* is intransitive in the sentence *The children played in their room* but transitive in the sentence *Violet plays the violin*.

intrusive 'r': the *r* sound pronounced between words or syllables, when there is no *r* in the spelling (*I saw a film*).

invariable: a word which does not vary in form by inflection. Such words include nouns as *sheep*, which remains the same when used in the plural: we say *a sheep* and *a flock of twenty sheep*.

inversion: the reversal of the usual word order, used for rhetorical effect. It particularly refers to subjects and verbs. Inversion is used in questions by including an auxiliary verb before the subject of the main verb (*Have you checked the time yet?*) and in some negative sentences (*Never had she experienced such joy*).

Inversion frequently involves adverbial phrases of place (*Beyond the town grew multitudes of daffodils*). It is also found in conditional clauses that are not introduced by conjunction (*Had we had some more time we could have finished the job*). Frequently used for literary effect, it is easy to over-use (*Backward ran the sentences until reeled the mind*).

inverted commas, **quotation marks** or **quotes:** punctuation marks, either single (' ') or double (" "), depending upon house style, used to mark the beginning and end of a quoted passage. They can also be used instead of italic type in the titles of books, newspapers, magazines, plays, films, or musical works ('The Sunday Times'). Inverted commas can also be used to emphasise or draw attention to a particular word or phrase

(*Can anyone in the class spell 'punctuation' for me?*). If a phrase or passage is already contained within inverted commas, the opposite style should be used to quote within it (*'She asked if anyone in the class could spell "punctuation" for her'* or *"She asked if anyone in the class could spell 'punctuation' for her"*).

irony: an expression of meaning, often humorous or sarcastic, by the use of language of a different or opposite tendency (*Thank you for your support – your silence was a great help!*).

irregular adjectives: adjectives that do not conform to the usual rules in forming the comparative and superlative. Many adjectives add ~*er* for the comparative and add ~*est* for the superlative (*quicker / quickest, slower / slowest*). Other adjectives form their comparatives with *more* and their superlatives with *most*, as in *more beautiful / most beautiful*. Irregular adjectives do not form their comparatives and superlatives in either of these ways. Irregular adjectives include:

positive	*comparative*	*superlative*
good	better	best
bad	worse	worst
little	less	least
many	more	most

irregular plurals: the plural forms of nouns that do not form their plurals in the regular way.

Most nouns in English add *s* to the singular form to create the plural form (*boy / boys, girl / girls*). Some add *es* to the singular form to create the plural (*beach / beaches, church / churches*). Nouns ending in a consonant followed by *y* have ~*ies* as a regular plural ending (*berry / berries, fairy / fairies*). These different forms are all examples of regular plurals.

Irregular plurals include words that are different in form from the singular forms and do not simply add an ending (*child / children, man / men, mouse / mice, woman / women*). Some irregular plurals are formed by changing the vowel of the singular forms (*foot / feet, goose / geese, tooth / teeth*), while other irregular plural forms are formed by adding *en* (*ox / oxen*).

Some nouns ending in ~*f* form plurals ending in ~*ves* (*half / halves, loaf / loaves, wolf / wolves*), but some have alternative endings (*hoof* to either *hoofs* or *hooves*), and some form regular plurals unchanged, as in *roof* to *roofs*.

Certain irregular plural forms are the original foreign plural forms of words adopted into English (*criterion / criteria, larva / larvae, phenomenon / phenomena, stimulus / stimuli*). This group includes *datum / data*, although the singular form is very rarely used. Currently there is a growing tendency to anglicise the plurals of foreign words as though they were English. Many of these co-exist with the plural form (*formulas / formulae*). Sometimes the anglicised plural formed according to the regular English rules differs slightly in meaning from the irregular foreign plural; thus *indexes* usually applies to guides in books and *indices* is mostly used in mathematics. Some nouns have irregular plurals in that the plural form and the singular form are the same. These include *sheep*, and *salmon*. Some nouns have a regular plural and an irregular plural form; thus *brother* has the plural forms *brothers* and *brethren* although the latter is now mainly used in a religious context and is archaic in general English.

irregular sentence: *see* **major sentence**.

irregular or **strong verbs:** do not conform to the usual pattern of verbs, that is, some of their forms deviate from what one would expect. There are four main forms of a **regular verb**:

- the infinitive or base form, as in *kick*;
- the third-person singular form, as in *he kicks*;
- the ~*ing* form or present participle, as in *kicking*;
- the ~*ed* form or past tense or past participle, as in *kicked*.

Irregular verbs deviate in some way from this pattern, in particular from the pattern of adding ~*ed* to the past tense and past participle. They fall into several categories.

One category concerns those which have the same form in the past tense and past participle forms as the infinitive and do not end in ~*ed*, like regular verbs. These include:

infinitive	*past tense*	*past participle*
bet	bet	bet
burst	burst	burst
cast	cast	cast
cost	cost	cost
cut	cut	cut
hit	hit	hit
hurt	hurt	hurt
let	let	let
put	put	put
run	run	run
set	set	set
shed	shed	shed
shut	shut	shut
slit	slit	slit
split	split	split
spread	spread	spread

Some irregular verbs have two past tenses and two past participles which are the same, as in:

infinitive	past tense	past participle
burn	burned, burnt	burned, burnt
dream	dreamed, dreamt	dreamed, dreamt
dwell	dwelled, dwelt	dwelled, dwelt
hang	hanged, hung	hanged, hung
kneel	kneeled, knelt	kneeled, knelt
lean	leaned, leant	learned, learnt
leap	leaped, leapt	leaped, leapt
learn	learned, learnt	learned, learnt
light	lighted, lit	lighted, lit
smell	smelled, smelt	smelled, smelt
speed	speeded, sped	speeded, sped
spill	spilled, spilt	spilled, spilt
spoil	spoiled, spoilt	spoiled, spoilt
weave	weaved, woven	weaved, woven
wet	wetted, wet	wetted, wet

Some irregular verbs have past tenses which do not end in ~ed and have the same form as the past participle. These include:

infinitive	past tense	past participle
become	became	became
bend	bent	bent
bleed	bled	bled
breed	bred	bred
build	built	built
cling	clung	clung
come	came	came
dig	dug	dug
feel	felt	felt
fight	fought	fought
find	found	found
flee	fled	fled
fling	flung	flung
get	got	got

infinitive	past tense	past participle
grind	ground	ground
hear	heard	heard
hold	held	held
keep	kept	kept
lay	laid	laid
lead	led	led
leave	left	left
lend	lent	lent
lose	lost	lost
make	made	made
mean	meant	meant
meet	met	met
pay	paid	paid
rend	rent	rent
say	said	said
seek	sought	sought
sell	sold	sold
send	sent	sent
shine	shone	shone
shoe	shod	shod
sit	sat	sat
sleep	slept	slept
slide	slid	slid
sling	slung	slung
slink	slunk	slunk
spend	spent	spent
spin	spun	spun
stand	stood	stood
stick	stuck	stuck
sting	stung	stung
strike	struck	struck
string	strung	strung
sweep	swept	swept
swing	swung	swung
teach	taught	taught

infinitive	*past tense*	*past participle*
tell	told	told
think	thought	thought
understand	understood	understood
weep	wept	wept
win	won	won
wring	wrung	wrung

Some irregular verbs have regular past tense forms but two possible past participles, one of which is regular. These include:

infinitive	*past tense*	*past participle*
mow	mowed	mowed, mown
prove	proved	proved, proven
sew	sewed	sewn, sewed
show	showed	showed, shown
sow	sowed	sowed, sown
swell	swelled	swelled, swollen

Some irregular verbs have past tenses and past participles that are different from each other and different from the infinitive. These include:

infinitive	*past tense*	*past participle*
arise	arose	arisen
awake	awoke	awoken
bear	bore	borne
begin	began	begun
bid	bade	bidden
bite	bit	bitten
blow	blew	blown
break	broke	broken
choose	chose	chosen
do	did	done
draw	drew	drawn
drink	drank	drunk
drive	drove	driven
eat	ate	eaten

infinitive	*past tense*	*past participle*
fall	fell	fallen
fly	flew	flown
forbear	forbore	forborne
forbid	forbade	forbidden
forgive	forgave	forgiven
forget	forgot	forgotten
forsake	forsook	forsaken
freeze	froze	frozen
forswear	forswore	foresworn
give	gave	given
go	went	gone
grow	grew	grown
hew	hewed	hewn
hide	hid	hidden
know	knew	known
lie	lay	lain
ride	rode	ridden
ring	rang	rung
saw	sawed	sawn
see	saw	seen
rise	rose	risen
shake	shook	shaken
shrink	shrank	shrunk
slay	slew	slain
speak	spoke	spoken
spring	sprang	sprung
steal	stole	stolen
stink	stank	stunk
strew	strewed	strewn
stride	strode	stridden
strive	strove	striven
swear	swore	sworn
swim	swam	swum
take	took	taken
tear	tore	torn

infinitive	*past tense*	*past participle*
throw	threw	thrown
tread	trod	trodden
wake	woken	woke
wear	wore	won
write	written	wrote

~**ise** and ~**ize**: both verb endings mean *to make* or *to become such* (*realise*); *to treat in such a way* (*pasteurise*); *to follow a special practice* (*economise*); *to have a specified feeling* (*sympathise*); *to effect* (*oxidise*). In British English especially, ~*ise* is in common use and is obligatory in certain cases such as *advertise, franchise, improvise*, often where it forms part of a larger word element such as ~*mise*, as in *compromise*, and ~*prise*, as in *enterprise, surprise*, and in verbs corresponding to nouns with ~*is*~ in the stem, as in *supervise, televise*. The ~*ize* form should be used with the stems of nouns ending in ~*ism* (*criticize*) or with complete nouns (*canalize*) but today the ~*ise* form is prevalent in British English even in words in which ~*ize* was previously considered mandatory (*agonise, appetise, civilise*) and so there are many verbs which can be spelt in either way (*computerise / ize; economise / ize; finalise / ize; hospitalise / ize; modernise / ize; organise / ize; realise / ize; theorise / ize*); *see also* ~**yse**.

~**ish**: a suffix indicating *having the qualities or characteristics of* (*biggish, boyish*), or *of the nationality of* (*British, Danish, Spanish*).

~**ism**: a suffix indicating an action or its result, as in *baptism*; a system, doctrine, principle or ideological movement, as in *Catholicism*; a state or quality, as in *heroism*; a basis of prejudice or discrimination, as in *racism*; a pathological condition, as in *alcoholism*; or even a characteristic or peculiarity of language, as in *Americanism*.

iso~: a prefix indicating *equal*, as in *isometric*.

~ist: usages of this suffix are so many and various that a full discussion of them is not possible here. However, its most widespread meaning is probably *believer*, *supporter* or *someone concerned with something*, as in *atheist, fascist, motorist, tobacconist*.

it: the neuter gender third-person pronoun, also often used as the subject of a sentence in the absence of a meaningful subject; *it* is commonly used in reference to time or the weather, as in *It is now midnight*; *It is beginning to rain*.

italics: a sloping, gracefully curved and flowing typeface that is commonly used to differentiate a piece of text from the main text, which is usually in Roman type; it should not be confused with the sloped version of the Roman face, which is identical with the original letterforms except for the angle from the vertical, which is the same for every letter. This angle may be different for each letter in an italic alphabet.

It is used to distinguish titles such as those of books, films, magazines, musical works, newspapers, and plays. The names of ships and trains, Latin names for plants and animals, and sometimes the names of fictional characters (He was reading about the *Cercis siliquastrum* in his copy of *The Times*, whilst travelling on *The Flying Scotsman* to Edinburgh).

Italic type is also used to indicate that the word or phrase is not English (My daughter was able to phone ahead on her mobile, *en route* to her new teaching job in France, to let them know that her flight had been delayed at Heathrow).

It can also be used for emphasis, to draw attention to one word or phrase that makes the point (Is he *still* in the pub?), or to accentuate the fact that a word is in sharp contrast to the expected one (Dr Johnson's best-known dictum is that second marriages are the triumph of *hope* over experience rather than *love*).

It can draw attention to two words in sharp contrast (If the child never *can* have a dull moment, the man never *need* have one). It is also used to isolate a word from the sentence (Here *will* is wrongly used instead of *shall*).

If the sentence is read aloud, the word in italics is accentuated (He knows that if *he* loses, there is no consolation prize of conscience awaiting *him*).

~**ite:** a suffix which indicates that *a person* or *thing is connected with* (*Israelite, Trotskyite, graphite, sulphite*).

~**itis:** a suffix indicating *illness* or *disease*, as in *bronchitis, appendicitis*.

its and **it's:** are apt to be confused. *Its* is a possessive determiner meaning *belonging to it* (*The dog has not eaten its dinner*). *It's* means *it is* or *it has* (*Can you believe it's finished?*).

~**ize:** *see* ~**ise**; *also* ~**yse**.

jargon: the technical or specialist language used among members of a specialist profession or group. Therefore, jargon should be avoided in any document or situation intended to be read by lay people who have no specialist knowledge of the subject under discussion, or of the language associated with it, unless each term is explained as it occurs or a glossary is appended. Jargon may even be used intentionally in order to obscure meaning, and then all too often it is utterly impenetrable to any member of the public who might come into contact with it; in some professions it easily becomes **gobbledygook**. Thus jargon has come to have a secondary meaning, being used as a derogatory term to describe generally any unnecessarily obscure or pretentious language, whether used within a profession or not.

journalese: derogatory term for a hackneyed style of language thought to be characteristic of some newspaper writing. It usually encompasses a style of writing that through either laziness or cynicism is characterised by short sentences that include extensive use of clichés and sensational language, or incorporate a very fresh and creative use of vocabulary: *see* **headline**.

jussive: a type of clause or sentence that expresses a command: *Do hush! I'm trying to listen.*

just: an adverb which indicates that something happened a short time previously. In British English it is usually used with the perfect tense of the verb: *I have just opened a fresh bottle.*

In American English, and more commonly with some speakers of British English, *just* may accompany the past tense of the verb, especially in an informal context: *I just had to go downstairs to see who was at the front door.*

Just has more than one meaning. It can mean *only*, but in this context care should be taken to position it in the correct place in the sentence. For example, in the sentence *He drank just two glasses of wine*, it means that he drank only two glasses of wine, but in the sentence *He just drank two glasses of wine* it means that he very recently drank two glasses of wine.

Just can also mean *exactly*, as in *That's just what I need*; it may also mean *fair* or *appropriate*.

justification: the spacing of words and letters within a line of printed text so that all full lines in a column have an even margin to both left and right. This entry has been set justified to the full type width on the page, although all other entries in this book are unjustified.

kenning: in Old Norse / English poetry, an expression incorporating two elements instead of using a single noun, or a vivid figurative description.

kilo~: a prefix denoting *a thousand*, *a factor of 1,000*, as in *kilogram*.

~kin: a suffix which indicates *a diminutive or smaller version*, as in *mannikin* for *small man* and in proper names, as in *Jenkin* from *John*.

kind: used as a noun to refer to a race or species (*human kind*), a natural group of animals or plants, or the class, type, sort or variety of something (*What kind of house do you live in?*). Since it is a countable noun, it should take the plural form *kinds* after words such as *all* and *many* (*At the zoo we saw animals of all kinds*). A singular noun should follow *kinds of* (*We have all kinds of house on the new estate*), but often people use a plural noun instead (*We have all kinds of houses here*), especially in informal speech.

These and *those* can cause grammatical problems. They are often used before *kind of*, as in *I prefer these kind of flowers*, but this is never correct and *this* and *that* should be used instead, as in *I prefer this kind of flowers*.

The use of *kind of* to mean *to some extent* or

rather, as in *I kind of expected it*, is frequent in American English, informal speech or dialect. This phrase is sometimes written *kinda*, as in *I kinda expected it*.

Kind is also used as an adjective, to mean *friendly*, *generous* or *of a gentle nature*, as in *Granny was a kind old soul, she always gave us sweets when we went to visit her*.

kindly: looks like an adverb but it can be either an adverb or an adjective. As an adverb it means *in a kind or caring manner* or *generously*, as in *She spoke kindly to the child*. The adverb *kindly* is also used in a polite request or demand: *Could you very kindly let me know when you have been able to make up our order*, or often in an ironic way when the user is annoyed: *Would you kindly leave me alone*. It is also used in the phrase *not to take kindly to*, meaning *to be unwilling to accept*, as in *My mother-in-law did not take kindly to our neighbour's dogs barking all night*.

Kindly is more common as an adjective and means *kind, warm, friendly*, as in *a kindly old man who would not hurt a fly*.

kneel: one of several verbs in English which have more than one past participle and past tense form. Both may be either *kneeled* or *knelt*, and although both *knelt* and *kneeled* are acceptable forms in British English, *knelt* is the more common form while in American English it is rare. In British English the choice is usually made on the basis of sound: *They knelt together in prayer*; *The congregation kneeled*; *They had knelt there for some time*; *Those in front had kneeled so as to give those at the back a better view*.

knowledge about language (KAL): in British educational linguistics, KAL represents the monitoring of the structure and function of spoken and written language by children as they progress through the school curriculum.

koine: the common language of the Greeks from the close of the Classical era to the Byzantine era. In modern usage it refers to a common language that is shared by various peoples; a *lingua franca* such as Mandarin Chinese.

labial: requiring partial, or complete, closure of the lips in the articulation of a sound.

labialization: the rounding of the lips while making a speech sound, as for the *oo* in *moon*.

labiodental: a speech sound made by using the lips and teeth.

labiovelar: a speech sound made by using the lips and the soft palate.

laid and **lain:** are apt to be confused. *Laid* is the past tense and past participle of the verb *to lay*, meaning *to place* or *to put*, as in *He laid the book on the table*. *Lain* is the past participle of the verb *to lie*, meaning *to rest in a horizontal position*, as in *That lazy good-for-nothing has lain in bed all morning*.

laconic: a style of speech or writing that is brief, concise or terse.

laminal: a consonant sounded with the blade (or *lamina*) of the tongue, in contact with the upper lip, teeth, or alveolar ridge.

language: the method of human communication, either spoken or written, consisting of the use of words in accordance with an agreed convention. *Language* can also refer to the form of communication used by a particular group or nation. The language that a person speaks from birth is known as his or her first language, or mother tongue, and he or she is said to be a native speaker of this language.

Language can also be used to refer to the style or the facility (or indeed felicity) of expression, of a piece of writing: *The translator's language is very poetic*. Language may also be used to refer to the specialised vocabulary that is used in a particular profession or among a particular group of people with some common interest, as in *legal language*, *technical language*. Such specialist language is sometimes referred to as **jargon** or (for example) as *legalese*; *see* **journalese**.

A person's own style of language in respect of vocabulary and structure is known as **ideolect**, and the language of a region or community with regard to vocabulary, structure, grammar and pronunciation is known as **dialect**.

Language may also be used to refer to a system of symbols and rules such as that for writing computer programs or algorithms.

last: may be an adverb or an adjective. As an adjective it can give rise to ambiguity. It may mean *coming after all others*, *coming at or belonging to the end* or *final*, as in *He was the last person to register his claim*. The ambiguity arises when *last* takes on other meanings: for example, it is frequently used as a synonym for *latest* or *most recent*, as in *I really enjoyed his last film, last Christmas*. In this particular sentence we assume that *last* means *most recent* not *final* in both cases, but this need not necessarily always be so; thus it is better to use either *final* or *latest* rather than *last*, in order to clarify the meaning.

Confusion can arise also between *last* meaning *final* and *last* meaning *preceding* or *previous in sequence*, as in *He got off at the last station*. On the evidence of the sentence alone, it is not clear whether *last* refers to the preceding station or to the final station; again, it is best to avoid ambiguity by using a synonym for *last*.

Last is also used as an adverb to mean *after all others*, as in *last-mentioned*, and *on the last occasion before the present*, as in *When did you last see him?*. Such adverbial use does not suffer from problems of ambiguity.

latest: an adjective that is apt to be confused with *last*. When preceded by *the* it may mean *fashionable* or *most up-to-date*, as in *the latest designs from Paris*. It can also mean *most late*, the superlative of *late* in the sense of *far on in time*, as in *I'll catch the latest train I can*. In this sense *latest* is also found in the phrase *at the latest* and in the phrase *at the very latest*, meaning *most late time*, as in *We have to leave at at ten o'clock at the very latest, if we are to arrive at the station in time*.

latinate: a term applied to any grammar that is based on the character of Latin.

lay *and* **lie:** are apt to be confused. This is because *lay*, as well as being a verb in its own right, is also one of the principal parts of *to lie* – the past tense, as in *The books lay on the table*.

Lay is a transitive verb meaning *to place or put*, as in *She asked him to lay the new carpet in the hall*. The principal parts of *lay* are:

- *lays* – third person singular present, as in *She always lays an old blanket in the cat's basket at night*;
- *laying* – present participle, as in *Laying down her book, she got up to make a cup of tea*; and
- *laid* – past participle and past tense, as in *She laid out the contents of her handbag on the table*.

Lie is an intransitive verb meaning *to recline*

horizontally, the principal parts of which are:

- *lies* – third person singular present, as in *Their village lies in a valley*;
- *lying* – present participle, as in *Lying on the sofa, both children soon fell asleep*;
- *lay* – past tense, as in *The sheepdogs lay on the grass, quiet but alert, until the trials began*; and
- *lain* – past participle, as in *Those bricks have lain there unused for absolutely ages*.

Lie has another totally unrelated meaning. It means *to say or write something that is untrue*, as in *She lied about the cost of the new carpet because it was well over their budget*. The principal parts of the verb *to lie* are:

- *lies* – third person singular present, as in *He lies about where he goes when playing truant*;
- *lying* – present participle, as in *You are lying to me about the severity of your symptoms*; and
- *lied* – past participle and past tense, as in *He lied to his father about what time he had got in*.

leading: the white space between lines of type.

lean: one of several verbs in English which have two forms of the past tense and the past participle, *leaned* and *leant*, as in *She leaned over to whisper to her classmate*; *He leant down to pick up the pencil*. In British English, the two forms are interchangeable, although the latter is unusual in American English.

leap: one of several verbs in English which have two forms of the past tense and past participle, *leaped* and *leapt*, as in *The children leapt into bed on the promise of a story*; *The horses all leaped over the fence and trotted briskly down the road*. The two forms are virtually interchangeable but *leapt* is more common in British English.

learn: one of several verbs in English which have

two forms of the past tense and past participle, *learned* (pronounced as one syllable, *lernd*) and *learnt*: *They learned how to do it properly*; *I have learnt my lesson*). The forms are interchangeable. *Learned* as a past tense or past participle should not be confused with *learned* (pronounced as two syllables, *ler-ned*), the adjective meaning *erudite*, *well-read* or *intellectual*, as in *He was considered a learned and distinguished man*.

length mark: *see* **macron**.

lenis: derived from the Latin and meaning *soft*, it is used to denote consonants made with a relatively weak degree of muscular effort and little breath force.

lenition: a relaxation of muscular effort during articulation, which can lead to a consonant being lost.

lento: said of a speech produced slowly or with careful articulation.

~less: a suffix meaning *not having*, *without*, *free from* or *lacking in* that can be added to nouns to form adjectives, as in *characterless*, *doubtless*, *fearless*. It can also be added to verbs to form adverbs meaning *not affected by* or *without being able to be measured*, as in *ageless*, *tireless*.

less: *see* **fewer**.

~let: a suffix indicating a diminutive or smaller form of something, as in *booklet*, *flatlet*, *droplet*, *leaflet*, or denoting articles of ornament or dress, as in *bracelet*, *anklet*)

letter: any of the symbols used in an alphabetic system of writing to represent one or more speech sounds.

letter-writing: has become something of a dying art in view of the widespread use of the telephone, and conventions have already begun to undergo further changes with the increasing use of e-mail. However, from time to time everyone has to write some form of letter and many of these are business letters. There are a few conventions in formal letters: your own address, including the postcode, should be placed at the right-hand side of the page. For handwritten letters, traditionally each line of this address was indented slightly below the one above and the date positioned below the last line:

15 Station Street
Readback
Middleshire
MA1 3QA

18 June 2001

Whether a comma should be included at the end of each line of the address is now a matter of taste; however, it is becoming less usual, and as postcodes were introduced into the UK so as to facilitate automatic sorting, a full point at the end of an address (which now ends with the post code) could result in a misreading by the computer, and so is best omitted.

The telephone number may be placed either between the postcode and the date, or at the other side of the page on the same line as the first line of the address.

When writing a business letter, you should also put the address of the person to whom you are writing. It should be placed at the other side of the page below your own address and the lines of this should be aligned on the left, placed directly below each other:

15 Station Street
Readback
Middleshire
MA1 3QA

18 June 2001

The Manager
Daylight Laundry
176 High Street
Oxbridge
Middleshire
MR8 7NY

It is best to find out the name of the person to whom you are writing whenever possible, which avoids having to use a very formal style of address, and instead you can start the letter off:

Dear Mr Castle,

Note that a comma is placed after the person's name, even when none has been inserted at the end of each line of the address.

When you are writing to a woman, the situation is slightly less clear. It used to be considered acceptable to address her as *Miss* if you knew her to be unmarried or if you did not know her marital status, or as *Mrs* if you knew her to be married. Alternatively you could use *Madam*, but this convention may now be regarded as unnecessarily formal, and *Ms* is the acceptable term if you know her name, but not her marital status. It is especially useful as a neutral means of addressing divorcées, and many younger women in particular prefer to be addressed in this way. It does afford a degree of privacy, in that really it should be of interest to no-one but her friends and family, whether she is married or not. Many married women, however, feel that *Mrs* confers more status or dignity than *Ms*.

Recently a convention has evolved of putting the first name and surname of the addressee instead of the surname preceded by title:

Dear David Castle,

This is quite informal, but less so than the complete omission of the surname, when the addressee is not personally known to the writer. This form has been promoted by large companies or organisations attempting to appear friendly, and on the same level as the recipient, but many find it impertinent if not actually offensive.

If for some reason it is not easy to find out the name of the person to whom you wish to write, then it is perfectly acceptable to address him or her in terms of the office held:

Dear Personnel Manager,

although it is more common in formal letters to use *Sir* or *Madam*:

Dear Sir,

Dear Madam,

When you do not know the sex of the person to whom you are writing, you may use either:

Dear Sir or Madam,

Dear Sir / Madam,

In ending a letter which addressed the person written to as *Dear Sir*, *Dear Madam*, or either of the non-specific *Dear Sir or Madam* or *Dear Sir / Madam* forms, it was traditionally the custom to write *Yours faithfully* before the signature:

Yours faithfully,

Janet Brown

If the letter was either informal in nature or a formal letter which addressed the person by name, it was customary to end the letter:

Yours sincerely,

Janet Brown

If the letter has been typewritten or produced on a computer, as signatures are rarely clearly legible it is polite to type your name beneath the space left for your signature:

Yours sincerely,

Janet Brown

Janet Brown

Often now a letter is ended, incorrectly, with the less formal *Yours sincerely*, even if it was begun with the formal *Dear Sir*, or its related forms. Similarly, although it is usual to end informal communications such as faxes and e-mails with *Kind regards* if the addressee is known to you, this is too informal for a letter.

On the envelope the lines may be indented or not, according to taste. Each line, except the last one, may or may not be followed by a comma. However, in current usage there is an increasing tendency to punctuate as little as possible and the commas are frequently omitted:

The Manager
Daylight Laundry
176 High Street
Oxbridge
Middleshire
MR8 7NY

When known, the addressee's style or title (*The Personnel Manager*, *Mr*, *Mrs*, *Miss* or *Ms* + surname) should be used on the envelope as in the opening greeting of the letter, *see above*.

Less formally, it is becoming increasingly common to write the full name of the addressee on the envelope:

Janet Brown
15 Station Street
READBACK
Middleshire
MA1 3QA

More formally, it has only ever been correct to use *Esq.*, usually spelt with a full stop at the end and preceded by a comma, if the man's family has a coat of arms. It was once used as a sort of flattery, but now is widely regarded as old-fashioned. If it is used, *Esq.* should be placed after the man's name and there should be no accompanying *Mr*:

John Brown, Esq.
15 Station Street
READBACK
Middleshire
MA1 3QA

Everything possible should be done to make the address absolutely clear. It is important always to use the postcode, as failure to do so slows down delivery of the letter. It is also preferable to highlight the post town, either by putting it in capital letters, or by underlining it:

The Manager
Daylight Laundry
176 High Street
OXBRIDGE
Middleshire
MR8 7NY

level *or* **rank:** in grammar, one of a series of structural layers within a sentence, clause, phrase, or word; in phonology, a degree of pitch, height or loudness during speech.

lexeme *or* **lexical item:** the smallest essential unit of a language comprising one or several words, the elements of which do not separately convey the meaning of the whole.

lexical diffusion: the gradual spread of a linguistic change through a language.

lexical, full *or* **main verb:** a verb expressing an action, event, or state.

lexicography: the art and practice of defining words, selecting them and compiling them in dictionaries and glossaries.

lexicology: the study of the form, history and meaning of a language's vocabulary.

lexicon *or* **lexis:** the vocabulary of a person, language or branch of knowledge, especially in dictionary form.

liaison: the pronunciation of an ordinarily silent final consonant before a word beginning with a vowel.

licence *and* **license:** are apt to be confused. *Licence* is a noun which means *a permit from an authority to own, use or do something*, as in *You need a licence to if you want to: watch your television / drive your car / marry / preach / sell alcoholic liquor*. *Licence* also means *permission, freedom to do something*, as in *License is a verb meaning 'to give licence to'*; it also means *liberty of action, lack of regard for rules of behaviour, social acceptability or morality*, as in *The licence the young people allowed themselves in their style of dressing was quite scandalous*. In this sense the word *licence* is most usually used in formal situations.

License as a verb means *to give official permission* or *authorisation to*, as in *He is licensed to sell produce from his allotment in the market on Tuesday*. *Licence* is often misspelt as *license* in British English, even when it is clearly a noun. However, in American English, *license* is used for both the noun and the verb.

lie: *see* **lay**.

ligature: refers to a printed character combining two or more letters in one, such as æ and œ. It is derived from the use in manuscripts of a small extra stroke used to join adjacent letters such as *ffi*, *lt*, which was continued in metal type when this was set by hand and even after it was set by machinery. Then the aim of the compositor setting the type was to make a close fit from the individual characters to give an even colour on the page between the black of the ink and the pale colour of the paper, without gaps or spots; *see also* **digraph**.

~like: a suffix meaning *similar to* or *characteristic of*, as in *childlike*, *doglike*, *lifelike*.

limerick: a humorous or comic form of five-line poem with the rhyme-scheme *aabba* – the first two lines rhyming with each other, the third and fourth lines rhyming with each other, and the fifth line rhyming with the first line. Usually there are three stressed beats in the first, second and fifth lines and two stressed beats on the third and fourth lines. Traditionally the name of a place is mentioned in the first line and may be repeated in the last line.Limerick is a town in Ireland, but the name of the verse is probably derived from the Victorian custom of singing or reciting improvised nonsense songs at parties. These often had the refrain *Will you come up to Limerick?* Edward Lear (1812–88) made the form popular in the nineteenth century. His *Book of Nonsense* offers:

> *There was a young lady of Ryde*
> *Whose shoe-strings were seldom untied*
> *She purchased some clogs*
> *And some small spotty dogs*
> *And frequently walked about Ryde.*

line-break: the division of a word at the end of a line in order to fill the space available, and is marked by a hyphen; *see* **hyphen**, **justification**.

~ling: a suffix indicating a diminutive (*duckling*),

or a person or thing connected with (*sapling*), or
having the property of being (*weakling*).

lingua franca: historically the term referred to a
language that was a mixture of Italian, French,
Greek, Spanish and Arabic, used for trading and
military purposes. Now it is used to refer to a
language that has been adopted as a common
means of communication between speakers
whose native languages are different, often for
shared purposes such as trading. Examples
include Hausa in West Africa, Mandarin Chinese
in Singapore, Swahili in East Africa, and Tok
Pisin in Papua New Guinea; *see also* **pidgin**.

lingual: any sound of, or formed by, the tongue.

linguist: someone who is proficient in several
languages or linguistics.

linguistics: the scientific study of language and its
structure. It describes language and seeks to
establish general principles rather than to
prescribe rules of correctness.

linguistic geography: *see* **geographical linguistics**.

linking adverbs and **linking adverbials:** words and
phrases which indicate some kind of connection
between one clause or sentence and another, such
as *however, in the meantime, instead, moreover,
then again: The bus was over thirty minutes late in
leaving. It did, however, make up most of the time*
en route; *We will not have a vacancy until next
week. In the meantime, I suggest that you take a
short holiday; I should have thought that he would
have given up by now. Instead he seems determined
to get to the end; He must be at least six feet tall.
Moreover, he's very solidly built; He does not have
much idea about gardening. Then again, his father
was unable to make anything grow.*

linking verb, **copula** *or* **copular verb:** a verb which connects a subject and a predicate. Unlike other verbs, linking verbs do not denote an action but indicate a state. The term copula refers to the verb *to be* and its various forms such as *become*. Examples of linking verbs include: *He appeared very happy*; *They became anxious*; *I felt disconcerted*; *He is a layabout*; *It is getting rather late*; *It is growing darker*; *She lived in a state of bewilderment*; *The poor child looks worried*; *You radiate enjoyment*; *She remained fearful for her friend*; *You seemed to be remarkably calm*; *The weather turned overcast*.

lipogram: a text from which a specific letter has been omitted throughout.

lisp: an articulation in which *s* is pronounced like *th* in *thick*, and / or *z* is pronounced as *th* in *this*. It is regarded as an impediment in English, but in other languages is received pronunciation.

literal meaning: the usual or primary sense of a word or phrase, without irony, subjective interpretation by the audience, or other literary devices being brought into play.

literary criticism: the art or practice of evaluating literary works and commenting on them.

litotes: a kind of ironical understatement, especially one in which a statement is conveyed by denying or contradicting its opposite: *It will be no easy task to repair the damage* means that the task will be a difficult one.

loan word: a word that has been taken into one language from another. From the point of view of the language taking the word in, the word is known as a borrowing; *see* **borrowing**. Some loan words become naturalised or fully integrated into the language and have pronunciations and spellings reflecting the conventions of the language which has borrowed them. Other loan words retain the spelling and pronunciation of the language from which they have been borrowed: *bête noire* has been borrowed from French and means literally *black beast*, but is used in English to describe a person or thing one particularly dislikes, dreads or fears, and for which there is no English equivalent word; *bugbear* is too weak.

localism: a word or expression which is used in a particular place or area. The area in question may be quite small, unlike those for **dialect** words or **regionalism**.

locative: the case of nouns, pronouns and adjectives that expresses location in languages that are inflected; in English, we have to use prepositions instead, as in *at the side, on top of the wardrobe*.

logogram, logograph: a written or printed sign representing a whole word in a language such as shorthand or in an ancient writing system such as heiroglyphics; also termed a character (only in Oriental languages); *but see also* **character**.

logogriph: a word puzzle using anagrams.

logorrhoea: the excessive, uncontrollable, perhaps incoherent, flow of words.

~logue: a suffix derived from Greek and meaning *talk, speech* as in *dialogue, travelogue, compilation*, as in *catalogue*, or *enthusiast*, as in *idealogue*.

long: a phoneme that contrasts because of its greater duration, as in the vowel of *beat* compared with *bit*.

look-and-say *or* **flash cards:** a method devised to teach reading to the very young, that focuses on the recognition of whole words which are written in large letters on individual cards that may be placed against the objects so named, like labels.

loudness *or* **volume:** the auditory sensation that primarily relates to a sound's intensity.

low: in phonetics, said of vowels made with the tongue in the bottom area of the mouth, and also of tones that use a relatively low pitch.

lower-case: small letters, as distinguished from capital letters. Lower-case letters are used for most words in the language, and capital letters are exceptional in their use; *see* **capital letters**.

~ly: a common adverbial ending; *see* **adverbs**.

macro~: a prefix derived from the Greek, meaning *large*, *large-scale* or *long*, as in *macroaxis*, *macrocosm*, *macrodactylous*, *macroeconomics*, *macrofauna*.

macron a mark used in phonetics in relation to a vowel to indicate that it is long or stressed (¯); a small horizontal stroke placed above a letter.

main clause: *see* **independent clause**.

major sentence: may be used to refer to a type of sentence that contains at least one subject and a finite verb (*He is fishing*; *We won*). They frequently have more elements than this (*He is going fishing next week*; *We won the match today*). Such sentences may be described as *regular* because they have certain structural patterns, for example a subject, finite verb, adverb.

The opposite of a major sentence, a *minor sentence*, is also known as an *irregular* or *fragmentary* sentence. Examples of these include interjections such as *Ouch!*, formulaic expressions such as *Good morning*, and short forms of longer expressions: *No dogs*. Such short forms could be rephrased to become major sentences: *The tenants' committee does not permit dogs in the garden*.

majuscules: a form of writing consisting of large letters, usually capitals, which are capable of being contained within a single pair of horizontal lines; this contrasts with *minuscules*, which are

small, usually lower-case, letters having
ascenders and **descenders** that would extend
above and below such lines.

mal~: a prefix derived from French meaning *bad,
unpleasant* (*malignant, malodorous, malpractice*),
or *faulty, imperfect* (*maladroit, malfunction*).

malapropism: the incorrect use of a word through
confusion with a similar-sounding word. It often
arises from an attempt to impress by the use of
long words or of technical language, and the
effect is often comic. In *I don't think that my
father's in full possession of all his facilities, facilities*
has been wrongly used instead of *faculties*.

Malapropism is called after Mrs Malaprop, a
character in R. B. Sheridan's *The Rivals* (1775).
Her name was derived from the French *mal à
propos*, meaning *not apposite, inappropriate*. One of
her coinages in the play is *She's as headstrong as
an allegory on the banks of the Nile*, where she has
used *allegory* instead of *alligator*. .

~man: formerly used with a noun as a stem to form
a noun indicating an official's function or a
person's job (*chairman, fireman, policeman*). Now,
as attempts are being made to purge sexism from
the language, alternatives have been sought for
any such words, which were often used whether
or not the person referred to was known to be a
man. Different suggestions have given us instead
chairperson or *chair, firefighter, police officer*.

~mania: a suffix denoting abnormal or obsessional
behaviour, as in *megalomania, nymphomania*.

manner: in phonetics, the specific process of
articulation used in a sound's production.

manner, adverbs of: *see* **adverb**.

manner, subordinate clause of: *see* **adverbial
subordinate clauses of manner**.

margins: sound segments that form the boundaries of a syllable.

masculine: of or denoting the gender proper to male persons or animals. It is the opposite of *feminine*. Nouns in the masculine gender include words that obviously belong to the male sex, such as *boy, schoolboy, man, salesman*. Many words now considered to be of dual gender were formerly assumed to be masculine, such as *author, engineer; see* **gender**. The masculine gender demands the use of the appropriate pronoun, including *he, him, his* and *himself; see* **he, she**.

mass noun: *see* **uncountable noun**.

~**mate:** a suffix identifying a *fellow member* or *joint occupant*, as in *classmate, flatmate, team-mate*.

me: *see* **I**.

medium: the means by which something, especially speech, is transmitted.

mega~: a prefix derived from Greek, and meaning *great*, as in *megabyte, megahertz, megapixel*. Many words using *mega~* in this way are of recent origin and many of them are also informal or slang. In technical language, *mega~* denotes a factor of 1 million (10^6) in the metric system of measurement.

meiosis: a figure of speech using understatement to emphasise the size or importance of something: *He's quite capable on the tennis court* means that he is, if not brilliant, far more than competent.

melted *and* **molten:** are apt to be confused. *Melted* is the past tense and past participle of the verb *to melt*, as in *The snowman had melted by the time they woke up in the morning*.

Molten is used only as an adjective; it is not synonymous with *melted*. Molten rock, metal or glass has been made liquid by subjecting the material to very high temperatures, as in *the molten rock was ejected from the erupting volcano*.

merger: in historical linguistics, the fusing together of linguistic units that were originally distinguishable.

meta~: a prefix derived from Greek and denoting *with* or a *change of position* or *condition*, or *beyond*, as in *metacarpal, metamorphosis, metaphysical*.

metanalysis: a word derived from a word-boundary error, as in *a nadder up* for *an adder-up*.

metaphor: a figure of speech in which one thing is compared to another without the use of *like* or *as* to make the comparison obvious: *He is the Hercules of the family; His dog is an awkward customer at the best of times; It's difficult to strike a balance; Life is a bowl of cherries; The craze was at its height last summer*. By extension, metaphor refers to a word or phrase used in a sentence where it does not have a literal meaning: *the European wine lake; the neighbour from hell; a private eye; see also* **mixed metaphor** *and* **simile**.

metathesis: the transposition of sounds or letters in a word, for example *anenome* for *anemone; ax* for *ask* in American English; *irrevalent* instead of *irrelevant*.

~meter: a suffix denoting *a measuring instrument*, as in *barometer, speedometer, thermometer*.

metonymy: a figure of speech in which the name of an attribute or adjunct is substituted for that of the thing meant: *the City* for *the people who work in London's financial sector, the Crown* for *the monarch, the Kremlin* for *the Russian government, the turf* for *horse-racing, the White House* for *the President of the United States*.

metre / meter *or* **measure:** any form of poetic rhythm, determined by the number and length of feet in a line; *see* **hexameter**, **iamb**, **pentameter**, **tetrameter**.

~metric: a suffix that forms adjectives corresponding to nouns that end in *~meter*, as in *thermometric* and *~metry*, as in *geometric*.

metrical: of, relating to, or composed in metre.

metrics: the study of metrical structure.

micro~: a prefix derived from Greek and meaning *very small*, as in *microchip*. In technical language, *micro~* denotes *a factor of 1 millionth* (10^{-6}), as in *microgram*, in the metric system of measurement.

mid: a vowel which is articulated between high and low tongue positions.

milli~: a prefix derived from Latin, and denoting a factor of one thousand, as in *millibar*, *milligram*.

mini~: a prefix meaning *very small* or *minor of its kind*, as in *minimum*, *minimal*, *minimise*. It is an abbreviation for *miniature* and has been widely used recently: *minibus*, *miniseries*, *miniskirt*.

minim: a single downstroke of the pen.

minimal pair: words that differ in meaning when only one sound is changed, as in *fit / sit*.

minor sentence: *see* **major sentence**.

minuscules: *see* **majuscules**.

mis~: a prefix added to verbs and verbal derivatives, and indicating *amiss*, *badly*, *wrongly* or *unfavourably*, as in *mislead*, *mistrust*. It also occurs in a few words adopted from French and meaning *badly* or *having a negative force*, as in *misadventure* and *mischief*.

misnomer: the incorrect or unsuitable use of a name or term.

mixed metaphor: the combination of inconsistent metaphors, as in *By sitting on the fence you are just burying your head in the sand*; *That prospect is the one oasis of hope in the sea of economic* *gloom; The company's new flagship did not get off the ground; They were caught red-handed with their trousers down.*

modal verb: a type of auxiliary verb that is used to express the mood of the main verb, and indicate such meanings as ability, certainty, necessity, permission, possibility, probability, suggestions, wants and wishes. The main modal verbs are *can* (*You can read my book; Can you find the time to look for it for me?*), *could* (*He could go if you paid*), both expressing ability; *could* (*Could you give me a hand?*) expressing instructions and requests; *may* (*You may answer when you're ready*) giving permission, *may* (*We may see her later after school*) or *might* (*We might get there in time for the start*), both expressing possibility; *might* (*You might like to think about the alternative*) offering a suggestion; *must* (*That must be a record price*) expressing certainty; *must* (*We must be ready for the taxi when it comes*) and *should* (*We should arrive at least one hour before the plane takes off*) expressing necessity; *shall* (*We shall leave my house in good time to catch the train*) expressing probability; *will* (*Will you have time to look in later?*) expressing an offer or invitation; *would* (*Would you take a note of the address for me?*) expressing a wish. Modal verbs have only one form. They have no ~*s* form in the third person singular, no infinitive and no participles.

modifier: a word, or group of words, used attributively that modifies or affects the meaning of another word in some way, usually by adding more information about it. Modifiers are frequently used with nouns. They may be adjectives (*He lives on the new estate*), but modifiers of nouns may also be nouns themselves (*the publishing industry*). They may also be place names (*the London underground*) or adverbs of place and direction (*a downstairs bar*).

Modifiers may also be used with adverbs (*running amazingly quickly*), adjectives (*a really sunny day*), and pronouns (*practically everyone present*). All these examples are pre-modifiers; *see also* **attributive adjective**, **post-modifier**.

~**monger:** a suffix derived from Old English which means *dealer* or *trader*, as in *fishmonger*, *ironmonger*. As well as being used for occupations in which people sell things, it is used in a derogatory manor to discribe people who promote or deal in less tangible things (*gossipmonger*, *rumourmonger*, *scaremonger*, *warmonger*).

mono~: a prefix derived from Greek, meaning *one*, *alone* or *single*, for example *monoacid*, *monocarpic*, *monochord*, *monochrome*, *monocle*, *monorail*.

monologue: speech or writing by a single person, in contrast with dialogue, in which two or more people are participants and interact.

monometer: a line of verse containing a single unit of rhythm.

monophthong: a single vowel sound.

monosyllabic: a word consisting of a single syllable.

monotone: speech or song continuing or repeated on one note without change of pitch.

months of the year: must always be spelt with initial capital letters (*January*, *February*, *March*, *April*, *May*, *June*, *July*, *August*, *September*, *October*, *November* and *December*).

mood: a form or set of forms of a verb. These moods in English are the indicative, imperative and subjunctive. They indicate the 'viewpoint' of the verb, whether it is expressing fact, the most usual form (indicative mood, as in *He runs in the*

New York marathon every year); command (imperative mood, *Go home at once, you bad dog!*) hypothesis (subjunctive mood, *If wishes were horses, beggars would ride*) or wish (subjunctive mood, *God save the Queen*); *see also* **subjunctive**.

more: an adverb which is added to some adjectives and adverbs to make the comparative form; *see* **comparative adjectives**, **comparative adverbs**.

morpheme: the smallest unit of grammar that cannot be further divided and is meaningful on its own: *in* and *come* are morphemes, which may be used together to form *income*.

morphology: the study of the forms of words, or the system of forms in a language.

most: an adverb which is added to some adjectives and adverbs to make the superlative form; *see* **superlative adjectives**, **superlative adverbs**.

mother tongue: the language that a person learns to speak first, as a native speaker.

mow: has two possible past participles, *mowed* and *mown*: *The gardener has not mowed the lawn yet*; *The lawn has been mown twice this week so far*. The two participles are interchangeable, but only *mowed* can be used as the past tense, as in *He mowed the grass yesterday*. *Mown* can also be an adjective: *I love the smell of freshly-mown hay*.

Ms, Mrs and **Miss:** *see* **letter-writing**.

multi~: a prefix derived from Latin, meaning *many* or *more than one*: *multiple*, *multiplicity*, *multiply*. *Multi~* is frequently used to form new words, such as *multi-media*, *multi-purpose*, *multi-role*.

multilingual: said of a person or group having a command of several languages.

multi-sentence : a sentence which has more than one clause, as in *She went up to her bedroom and turned on the light*.

mutation: in Celtic languages particularly, a change in the quality of the sound of a consonant because of the influence of a preceding word.

narrow: in phonetics, a detailed transcription, with each phoneme having a different symbol, distinguished by diacritical marks; *see* **diacritic**.

narrowing: in historical linguistics, a type of change in which a word becomes more specialised in meaning; for example, *mete* Old English for food / *meat*, a type of food.

nasality: in phonetics, a speech sound made with the soft palate lowered, thus allowing air to resonate through the nose.

native speaker: the speaker of a language as a first language or mother tongue.

~naut: a suffix derived from Greek, and meaning *navigator*, as in *aeronautical*, *astronaut*, *cosmonaut*.

negation: a process of contradiction or denial of some or all of the meaning of a sentence.

negative sentence: a sentence or statement expressing denial, as in *She does not have a dog*. The negative concept is expressed by an auxiliary verb accompanied by *not* or *n't*. Other words used in negative sentences include *never*, *nothing* and *by no means*, as in *I have never seen it*; *There is nothing to see*; *By no means can it be seen*.

neither: meaning not the one nor the other (of two things), as an adjective or a pronoun it takes a singular verb, as in *Neither teacher was present*. In the *neither ... nor* construction, *neither* introduces the first of two or more things in the negative, and a singular verb is used if both parts of the construction are singular, as in *Neither Bill nor Ben was present*. If both parts are plural the verb is plural, as in *Neither their parents nor their* *teachers were present.* If the construction involves a mixture of singular and plural, in speech the verb may agree with the subject that is nearest it, as in *Neither her teacher nor her parents are going to attend*; *Neither her teachers nor her mother is going to attend*, but in writing this is grammatically dubious, and it would be better to recast the sentence altogether in order to avoid the problem, as for pronouns.

neo~: prefix originating from the Greek, denoting a *new* or *revived form*: *Neoclassical*, *neo-Fascist*.

neologism: a word that has been newly coined (*moshing*, *yuppie*) or a familiar one used in a new sense (*greenhouse effect*, *happy-clappy*).

neur(o)~: a prefix derived from Greek, meaning *nerve* or *the nerves*, as in *neuralgia*, *neuroanatomy*, *neurobiology*, *neurogenic*, *neuropeptide*, *neurosis*.

neuter: one of the grammatical genders. The other two grammatical genders are *masculine* and *feminine*. In English, inanimate objects such as *bottle*, *cup*, *chair*, *table* are of the neuter gender.

neutralization: the loss of a contrast between two phonemes in a particular environment.

Newspeak: a language, especially of bureaucrats and politicians, that is full of ambiguities, jargon and propaganda. It derives from the language invented by George Orwell (1903–50) in his 1949 satirical novel *Nineteen Eighty-Four*.

nom de plume *or* **pseudonym:** a false name adopted by an author: *Mark Twain* for *Samuel Langhorne Clemens*. Theoretically, the term means *pen name* in French, though it was constructed in England; the French use *nom de guerre*, *war name*.

nomenclature: the system of terminology of a science.

nominal: a noun or noun-like item.

nominalisation: the formation of a noun from some other word class.

nominative: the case of nouns, pronouns and adjectives that typically identifies the **subject** of a verb; also sometimes called subjective.

nonce: an inventive or accidental linguistic word form, coined for one occasion. The prose of James Joyce and the verses of Dylan Thomas and Edward Lear offer many examples.

non-defining relative clause, **non-identifying relative clause** *or* **non-restrictive relative clause:** the kind of relative clause that is not essential to the sentence, because it only adds extra information about the noun it is related to, as in *I've just seen Mrs Smith, who wants to buy your car*, in which *I've just seen Mrs Smith* would make sense on its own, without the relative clause. Another example is *You see the old Rolls-Royce, over there on the right?*, where the relative clause *on the right* isn't essential to the sentence.

These clauses are less usual in conversation, because they are formal.

Non-defining relative clauses are separated from the rest of the sentence by one or two commas: *This is Mr Gallagher, who writes comic poetry*; *Dorothy, who cuts my hair, has moved to another hairdresser's*.

In non-defining relative clauses, as distinct from defining relative clauses, the relative pronoun *that* cannot be used, and object pronouns cannot be left out.

In a formal style, prepositions are put before the pronoun: *Universal Agroplastics, of which Max Harrison used to be the chairman, has made a loss of three million pounds this year*. In an informal style, prepositions can come at the end of the relative clause: *She spent all evening talking about her latest book, which none of us had ever heard of.*

non-finite clause: a clause which contains a non-finite verb. Thus in the sentence *He trains hard to earn a place*, the phrase *to earn a place* is a non-finite clause, since *to earn* is an infinitive and so a non-finite verb. Similarly in the sentence *Getting there was an expense*, the phrase *getting there* is a non-finite clause, *getting* being a present participle and so a non-finite verb.

non-finite verb: is one which shows no variation in tense and which has no subject. The non-finite verb forms include the infinitive form (as in *go*), the present participle and **gerund** (as in *going*), and the past participle (as in *gone*).

non-gradable: *see* **gradable**.

non-identifying relative clause: *see* **non-defining relative clause**.

non-restrictive relative clause: *see* **non-defining relative clause**.

non sequitur: an irrelevant remark lacking a logical connection with what has just been said, or a false deduction incorrectly derived from given information: *Born in Birmingham, he was fascinated by trains from the day of his birth.* The Latin phrase means literally *it does not follow*.

normative: descriptive of a linguistic rule which is considered to establish a socially approved standard of correctness, or norm, for language use.

notional: said of a verb conveying its own meaning, not auxiliary to another.

noun: a word, other than a pronoun, or group of words used to identify any of a class of persons, places or things (**common noun**), or a particular one of these (**proper noun**), as in *apple, arm, butcher, dog, foot, mouse, pear, shoe, sock, table.*

There are various categories of nouns; *see* **abstract noun**, **common noun**, **concrete noun**, **countable noun**, **proper noun** and **uncountable noun**.

noun group: *see* **noun phrase**.

noun phrase *or* **noun group:** a group of words that contains a noun as its main word and functions like a noun in the sentence. Therefore it can function as the subject, object or complement of a sentence. In the sentence *The large red car hit him*, the phrase *the large red car* is a noun phrase, and in the sentence *They bought a flat with a balcony*, the phrase *with a balcony* is a noun phrase. In the sentence *He is a total loss*, the phrase *a total loss* is a noun phrase.

nucleus: the syllable in a tone group that carries maximum pitch prominence.

number: in grammar, the classification of words by their singular or plural forms. Thus the number of the pronoun *they* is plural and the number of the verb *carries* is singular; *see* **agreement**.

number agreement: *see* **agreement**.

numbers: may be written in either figures or words. It is largely a matter of taste which method you should adopt; as long as the method is consistent within a piece of work, it does not really matter. Many establishments such as publishing houses or newspaper offices have a house style to which they will always conform. For example, numbers up to 10 are written in words: *I've got two pigs and three goats*, but greater numbers are written in figures. If this system is adopted, guidance should be sought as to whether a mixture of figures and words in the same sentence is acceptable, as in *There are 12 guests but only six chairs*, or whether the rule should be broken in such situations: *There are twelve guests but only six chairs*.

numeral: a figure, or group of figures denoting a number; used in grammar to distinguish figures from quantity, and generally more often for roman (i, ii, iii or I, II, III) than for arabic numbers (1, 2, 3).

obelisk *or* **dagger:** a typographical symbol, the functions of which include marking a cross-reference or, when used alongside a personal name, signalling that the person is dead.

object: in grammar, the object of either a verb or a preposition is the word or phrase which completes the structure begun by the verb or preposition.

There are two kinds of object of a verb, direct objects and indirect objects.

- The direct object of a transitive verb is the noun group which is used to refer to someone or something directly affected by or involved in the action performed by the subject.
- A direct object can be a noun, and in the sentence *They cut down the tree*, *the tree* is the object. In the sentence *I've just had a bath*, *a bath* is the object. In the sentence *Have you seen the neighbour today?*, *the neighbour* is the object.
- A direct object can be a noun phrase, and in the sentence *The old man told them a beautiful story*, *a beautiful story* is the object. In the sentence *I love this big house*, *this big house* is the object. In the sentence *Why do you always ask such silly questions?*, *such silly questions* is the object.
- A direct object can be a subordinate clause, and in the sentence *No one ever understands what he means*, *what he means* is the object. In the sentence *I couldn't say (that) I didn't enjoy*

it, (*that*) *I didn't enjoy it* is the object. In the sentence *I wonder when he intends to come back*, *when he intends to come back* is the object.

- A direct object can also be a pronoun, and in the sentence *I saw him*, *him* is the object. In the sentence *She knows them well enough to anticipate that!*, *them* is the object. In the sentence *Who doesn't love her?*, *her* is the object.

- Some sentences which contain a transitive verb, and therefore a direct object, also have an indirect object.

- An indirect object is an object which is used to indicate who benefits from an action or gets something as a result. The prepositions *to* and *for* precede the indirect object if it comes after the direct object, as in *I suggested a way out to her*, where *a way out* is the direct object, and *to her* is the indirect object. If the indirect object comes before the direct object, there is no preposition introducing it, as in *I can give you some*, where *some* is the direct object and *you* is the indirect object.

- An indirect object can be a noun, and in the sentence *I've just offered some help to my neighbour*, *to my neighbour* is an indirect object. In the sentence *Joe bought this ring for Sophie*, *for Sophie* is the indirect object.

- An indirect object can be a noun phrase, and in the sentence *I would like to pay you for what you have done*, *for what you have done* is the indirect object.

- An indirect object can be a pronoun, and in the sentence *Can you tell me that beautiful story?*, *that beautiful story* is the indirect object. In the sentence *I know you can do that for her*, *for her* is the indirect object.

- Some verbs can be used with a direct object, an indirect object, or both, for example *ask* (*I asked her*; *I asked what to do*; *I asked her what to do*); *owe*, *pay*, *show*, *teach*, and *tell*.

oblique: *see* **solidus**.

obsolescent: a word or usage which is dying out; going out of use.

obstruent: sounds made with a constriction; in phonetics, a **stop** or a **fricative**.

occlusion: the brief closure of the vocal passage during the articulation of a stop consonant.

octameter: a line of verse containing eight units of rhythm.

~oholic: *see* **~aholic**.

~ology: a suffix derived from Greek and indicating *study of*, as in *entomology*, *etymology*, *technology*.

omni~: a prefix derived from Latin and indicating *all* or *in all ways*, as in *omnipresent*, *omniscient*.

one: an impersonal way of saying *I*. It is used with the **third person** singular form of the verb: *One feels insulted*, not *One* [I] *feel insulted*. Its own pronouns should be used: *One prefers that one's own financial dealings are known only to oneself*. It may also be used to mean *anyone*, *an average person*, in which case it may be difficult to avoid a mixture of pronouns. In the sentence *One must understand that you just can't do that*, it would have been better to use the second-person *You* throughout. When it is used consistently the repetition may sound affected; now it is reserved for formal use and not much used in speech.

onomastics *or* **onomatology:** the study of the origin, formation and use of proper names.

onomatopœia: a figure of speech which uses words the sound of which reflects their meaning, as in *crackle*, *cuckoo! gurgle*, *purr*, *sizzle*, *whinny*.

onset: the consonants which precede the nucleus of a syllable.

open: in grammar, a word class with unlimited membership (noun, adjective, adverb, verb); in phonology, a syllable that ends in a vowel; in phonetics, vowels pronounced with a relatively wide opening of the mouth.

opposition: a linguistically important contrast between sounds.

oracy: ability to express oneself fluently in speech.

oral: sounds made in the mouth; those made in the nose are described as nasal; *see* **nasality**.

ordinal numbers: *first, second, third,* and so on, as distinct from **cardinal numbers** *one, two, three.*

orthoepy: the study of correct pronunciation.

orthography: correct or conventional spelling, or spelling according to accepted usage.

~osis: a suffix derived from Greek and indicating a *disease* or *condition*, as in *neurosis* and *thrombosis.*

over-correction: *see* **hypercorrection**.

oxymoron: a figure of speech linking apparently contradictory words: *the wisest fool in Christendom.*

palaeo~ *or* **paleo~:** a prefix derived from Greek and meaning *old* or *ancient*, as in *palaeontology.*

palaeography: the study of writings and inscriptions from the ancient past.

palatal: sounds made by placing the tongue in the area of the hard palate, for example the *y* in *yes.*

palatalization: an articulation in which the tongue moves towards the hard palate while another sound is being made.

palate: the arched bony structure that forms the roof of the mouth. It is divided into the hard palate towards the front, and the soft palate or *velum*, at the rear.

palato-alveolar: a consonant made between the alveolar ridge and the hard palate.

palindrome: a word, expression or even a whole sentence that reads the same backwards and forwards: *dad*, *noon*, *madam*, *reviver*, *rotator*, *nurses run*, *Able was I ere I saw Elba*, *Lewd did I live, & evil I did dwell* (which is cheating a bit).

pan~: a prefix derived from Greek and meaning *all* or *everywhere*, as in *panacea*, *pandemic*.

pangram: a sentence that contains every letter of the alphabet: *The quick brown fox jumped over the lazy dogs*.

paradigm: in grammar, a set of the inflected forms of a word; generally, an example or pattern.

paradox: an apparent absurd or contradictory statement that contains a truth.

paragram: a play on words by altering a letter, especially in humour: *He went to exercise* [*exorcise*] *the ghost*; intentional, unlike a **malapropism**.

paragraph: a subdivision of a piece of prose. It always begins on a new line, is usually indented from the margin and must contain at least one sentence. Many people find it difficult to divide their work into paragraphs. Learning to do so can be difficult but it is an area of style that improves with practice and writers develop an intuition as when to start a new paragraph.

In a report or discussion, the opening paragraph should introduce the topic. The closing paragraph should sum up the major points raised in the discussion and offer a brief conclusion. The paragraphs in between should deal with a single theme or point of the writer's writing or argument. When that has been dealt with, a new paragraph should be started.

However, there are other considerations to be

taken into account. If the paragraph is very long, not only might it be visually off-putting to the would-be reader, but it may also prove difficult for the reader to absorb or comprehend. In such cases it is best to sub-divide the themes and shorten the paragraphs.

A string of short paragraphs can create a disjointed, rather staccato effect which might not be what is intended. It is best to try to aim for a mixture of lengths to create some rhythm in the text and to tempt potential readers to read on.

Single-sentence paragraphs were once thought to be poor style, and unless you are Henry James reincarnated it is best to avoid long, complex sentences, but there are no hard and fast rules about this. Generally it takes more than just one sentence to develop a theme, but in specialised types of writing this does not necessarily apply. For example, a tabloid journalist or copywriter for an advertising firm must make the point very succinctly. For the treatment of dialogue in a work of fiction; *see* **dialogue**.

paralanguage: features elements other than words in speech, such as gesture and tone of voice, considered to be subordinate to language proper.

parallelism: the use of paired sounds, words, or constructions.

paraphrase: a free rendering or alternative version of a passage that does not change its meaning.

pararhyme: the repetition of the same initial and final consonants in different words, e.g. *fail / fall*.

parataxis: the placing of clauses or phrases in sequence but without using conjunctions to indicate their relationship: *I was late getting home last night, went straight to bed, didn't sleep* .

parenthesis: *see* **brackets.**

paronym: a word that comes from the same root as another, such as *wise / wisdom*, or has been formed from a foreign word; adjective *paronymous*.

parsing *or* **diagramming:** analysing and labelling the grammatical elements of a sentence.

participle: in traditional grammar, a word formed from a verb (*being, been*); also used in compound verb forms (*has been*), or as an adjective (*working woman*); *see* ~**ing, past participle**.

particle: a minor part of speech, with a grammatical function, which does not change its form, for example *to go, not*; also a common prefix or suffix such as *in*~, ~*ness* or a clause in a document.

partitive: denoting part of a collective group or quantity, as in *any, part-, piece, portion, some*.

passive voice: this verb form is used mainly in scientific work or to depersonalise or disguise the agent of the action.Essentially the subject and the object appear to change places in the sentence when the active verb form is changed to the passive form. In our example *The dog chased the cat*, the verb-form is in the **active voice**, because the subject, *The dog*, has performed the action *chased* on *the cat*, the object. By contrast, in *The cat was chased by the dog*, at the beginning of the sentence the 'subject' *The cat* didn't perform the action; *the dog* did, but the verb-form used, *was chased by*, expresses the action from the cat's point of view. This sentence and the verb-form used are said to be in the passive voice; *see also* **voice**.

past continuous: *see* **past progressive**.

past participle: formed by adding '~ed' or '~d' to the base word of regular verbs (*acted, handed, wanted*), or in various other ways for **irregular verbs**.

past perfect continuous: *see* **past perfect progressive**.

past perfect progressive: constructed with *had*, the

past tense of *to have* or *been*, the past participle of *to be*, and the present participle of the verb, as in *We'd been walking for hours*. It is used to describe situations that had been going on continuously up to the moment we are talking about.

past perfect simple *or* **pluperfect:** is constructed with *had*, the past tense of *to have*, and the past participle of the verb, as in *I had met him before last night*. If we are already talking about the past, we use the past perfect simple to go back to an earlier past time, to talk about things that had already happened at the time we are talking about. It is common in reported speech after verbs like *asked, explained, said, told* or *thought*, as in *I asked him if he had been there before*.

past progressive: made of the past tense of *to be* (*was / were*) with the present participle of the verb, as in *The sun was shining*. It is used to talk about what was already happening at a given moment in time. It is often used in sentences with verbs in the **past simple**. The past simple often refers to an event that interrupted the longer one referred to by the past progressive, as in *The phone rang while I was having my bath*.

past simple *or* **past tense:** a way of conjugating a verb to show that an event has already taken place. For example, the past tense of *to be* is *I was, you were, he / she / it was, we / you / they were*.

Most uses of the past simple refer to an action or situation which took place in the past, at a definite time, with a gap between its end and the moment of speaking. The time when it happened is known: *I went to Wales last summer*.

The past simple may be used to refer to the present time in reported speech. If I say, *I am hungry* and you are not listening, a moment later you might ask, *Did you say you were hungry?* meaning, *Are you hungry now?*

It is also used to express a hypothesis, or in a clause with *if …* : *I wish I had a pony of my own.*

It is also used in polite questions: *Did you want to leave?* rather than *Do you want to leave?*.

past tense: *see* **past simple**.

patois: a provincial dialect of the common people, differing quite fundamentally from the literary language of the region.

patronymic: a name derived from that of a person's father or ancestor, for example *Johnson*.

pejorative: said of a linguistic form that expresses a disparaging meaning (as in *goodish*).

pentameter: a line of verse containing five metrical feet; the commonest rhythm in English.

perfect *or* **preperfect:** *see* **present perfect**.

period *see* **full stop**.

periphrasis: the use of separate words instead of inflections to express a grammatical relationship; a roundabout way of speaking, as in *more hungry* instead of *hungrier*.

~person: *see* **~man**.

personal pronoun: used to refer back to someone or something that has already been mentioned. The personal pronouns are divided into subject pronouns, object pronouns and possessive pronouns. They are also categorised according to *person*; *see* **first person**, **second person**, and **third person**.

pharynx: the part of the throat above the larynx.

phonation: the utterance of sound through the use of the vocal folds.

phone: a simple speech sound.

phoneme: the smallest contrastive sound unit in the system of a language.

phonetics: the classification of speech sounds.

phonetic spelling: a spelling system that uses symbols for each individual speech sound.

phonics: a method of teaching reading based on the sounds of individual letters.

phonology: the study of sound systems of languages.

phrasal verb: an idiomatic phrase consisting of a verb and an adverb, as in *cut down*; a verb and a preposition, as in *go under*; or a combination of both, as in *press down on*.

phrase *or* **group:** a cluster of words smaller than a sentence, forming a grammatical unit, as in *my cherished dream, the white house*.

pictogram *or* **pictograph:** a symbol, used in picture writing, that represents a word or phrase.

pidgin: a simplified language composed from the vocabulary from two or more languages, developed for communication between people who do not share a common language.

pitch: the auditory sensation of the height of a sound.

pleonasm: the use of more words than necessary, perhaps for emphasis or rhetorical purposes, as in *to see with one's eyes*; *see also* **circumlocution, tautology**.

plosive: a consonant produced by the sudden release of air.

pluperfect: *see* **past perfect simple**.

plural noun: refers to *more than one* and is contrasted with **singular noun**. Singular nouns form their plurals in different ways. Most singular nouns add ~*s* (*bat / bats*), or they add ~*es* (*church / churches*). Singular nouns ending in a consonant followed by ~*y* add ~*ies* (*story / stories*); *see also* **irregular plural**.

point: *see* **full stop**.

polysemia *or* **polysemy:** the existence of several meanings of a word (*dull = stupid, boring, not sharp*).

polysyllabic: a word having more than one syllable.

possessive apostrophe: *see* **apostrophe**.

possessive pronoun: *see* **apostrophe**, **personal pronoun**, **first person**, **second person** and **third person**.

postalveolar: a consonant made at the rear of the alveolar ridge.

postdeterminer: a type of word which occurs after the determiner and before an adjective in a noun phrase (*the two large shops*).

post-modifier: comes after the main word of a noun phrase (*hearts of oak*).

postposition: a word with prepositional function which follows a noun or noun phrase.

predeterminer: a word that is used before a determiner, but is still part of the noun phrase. For example, *all* in *all the boats* and *both* in *both their boats* are predeterminers.

predicate: in certain systems of grammar, refers to all the parts of a clause or sentence that are not contained in the subject; what they tell us about the subject. Thus in the sentence *The small child was tired and hungry*, the phrase *was tired and hungry* is the predicate.

predicative adjectives: help to form the predicate and so come after the verb, like *tired* and *hungry* in *The small child was tired and hungry*.

prefix: a letter or group of letters, which is added to the beginning of a word in order to adjust or qualify its meaning. For example, the prefix *un~* is added to the adjective *happy* to form the adjective *unhappy*; *see* **affix**, **suffix**.

premodifiers: come before the main word of a noun phrase, as the adjective *red* in *red shoes*.

preperfect: *see* **present perfect**.

prepositional phrase: a component of structure that consists of a preposition followed by a noun phrase.

prepositions: words which link two elements of a sentence, clause or phrase together. They show how the elements relate in time or space and generally precede the words which they **govern**. Words governed by prepositions are nouns or pronouns. Prepositions are often very short words, such as *at, in, on*: *We were looking at his photograph*; *They sat in the back of the car*; *The cat sat on the mat*. Some complex prepositions consist of two words, such as *ahead of, apart from*: *The children walked ahead of the teacher*; others consist of three, such as *in addition to*: *I've got a four-wheel drive now, in addition to the estate*.

present continuous: *see* **present progressive**.

present participle: *see* **~ing words**.

present perfect, **perfect**, **preperfect** *or* **present perfect simple:** made of the present tense of the auxiliary *to have* followed by the past participle of the verb, as in *I have eaten*. It relates past actions and events to the present, looking back in time. It is grounded at the point *now*, the moment of speaking, and is used:

- To express unfinished past, as in *I've lived in Oxford for two years*; *He's been in this company since 1997*. The action began in the past and continues to the present. It usually refers to permanent actions and situations, while the **present perfect progressive** refers to more temporary actions and situations.
- To express experience, as in *Have you ever been to Canada?*; *I've had two accidents in my career as a racing driver*. The action happened in the past, but we don't know when or the time when it happened is not particularly relevant.

- To express the present result of a past event, as in *I've lost my purse. Have you seen it?*; *She's broken her ankle, so she can't play squash*. The action happened in the past, usually recently, and it has an effect in the present.

present perfect continuous: *see* **present perfect progressive**.

present perfect progressive: made of the present tense of the auxiliary verb *to have* followed by *been* (past participle of the auxiliary verb *to be*) and the present participle of the verb, as in *They've been going out together for years*.

Like the **present perfect**, the present perfect progressive looks back in time from the point *now*, the moment of speaking. It is used to talk about unfinished past actions and situations continuing up to the present: *I've been working all day*. Whereas the present perfect refers to permanent actions and situations, the present perfect progressive is used for rather temporary actions and situations.

present progressive: formed with the present tense of the auxiliary verb *to be* followed by the present participle of the verb: *I am going*. It is used to talk about temporary situations or actions that are already happening at the moment of speaking: *My sister is living at home for the moment*.

Events that will happen in the future may be described in the present progressive, and it implies that there is a plan or arrangement that has been made by somebody: *We're probably spending next weekend at home*.

It is sometimes used in narratives to set the scene or to give the context of the story: *'And there I'm sitting, minding my own business, when this guy walks over to me and ...'*.

The present progressive may also be used to express habits that are annoying, with such adverbs as *always*, *continually*, *forever*: *He's always leaving his shoes in the doorway*.

present simple *or* **present tense**: the most basic way of conjugating a verb. For example, the present tense of *to be* is *I am*, *you are*, *he / she / it is*, *we are*, *you are*, *they are*.

The present tense has different uses, three of them actually referring to the present. It is used for:

- Statements that are true all the time: *This jumper is green*; *Oil floats on water*.
- Habitual actions in the present: *I go to the gym every Friday*.
- Instantaneous present, when the action begins and ends around the moment of speech. It is frequent in sports commentaries: *... and Smith passes to Devaney ...*.

The present tense may also be used to talk about the future, to disassociate the speaker who views the event as being independent of perception or volition. It is used in referring to schedules: *The train arrives at 6.57*.

The present tense can also be used instead of the **present perfect**, in expressions like *I hear*, *I gather* or *I see*: *I hear you're getting engaged*.

Finally, the present tense is used to refer to temporary situations, with verbs which cannot be put in the continuous form: *I like this ice cream very much*.

presupposition: the information that a speaker assumes to be known beforehand.

preterite: the simple past tense form of a verb.

prevocalic: descriptive of a sound which precedes a vowel.

primary verb: a verb which can function either as a main verb or as an auxiliary verb: *be*, *have*, *do*.

principal clause: *see* **independent clause**.

progressive *or* **continuous** (**tense**): in grammar, said of a verb form that typically expresses an action in progress, as in *I am running*.

pronominal: an item that serves as a pronoun.

pronoun: a word that takes the place of a noun or a noun phrase; *see* **demonstrative pronoun**, **distributive pronoun**, **he**, **her**, **him**, **his**, **indefinite pronoun**, **interrogative pronoun**, **personal pronoun**, **reciprocal pronoun**, **reflexive pronoun** and **relative pronoun**.

prop word: *see* **empty word**.

proper noun: a noun which refers to a particular individual or specific thing. It is the name of someone or something, as in *Italy*, *Rome*, *the Vatican*, *Pope Paul*, *River Tiber*, *Mediterranean Sea*; *compare with* **common noun**; *see also* **capital letters**.

proposition: a unit of meaning in statement form that is asserted to be true or false, as in *The day follows the night*, *The dog is black*, *Today is Tuesday*.

proscriptive: prescriptive rules that forbid a usage, as in the injunctions not to end a sentence with a preposition (*She said that her new sofa was for sitting on, not looking at*) or to begin a sentence with a conjunction (*But it is such a beautiful day, how can you bear to stay indoors at the computer?*).

prosody: the study of speech rhythms.

prothesis: the addition of a letter or syllable at the beginning of a word (as in *be~* in *beheaded*).

proverb: a short, pithy, rhythmical saying in general use expressing a general belief: *All that glisters is not gold*; *Every cloud has a silver lining*; *Two wrongs don't make a right*.

pseudepigraphy: the false ascription of an author's name to a written work.

pseudonym: *see* **nom de plume**.

pun: a play on words which relies for its effect on the use of a word to suggest different meanings, or of words of the same sound and different meanings: *A flea met a fly in a flue; said the flea to the fly, Let us flee! So they flew through a flaw in the flue*.

punctuation: a set of graphic signs (, ; : . ' ' –) used in written language to indicate its structure, either to separate units in a linear sequence, to indicate when one unit is included in another, or to convey a specific grammatical or attitudinal function.

pure vowel: a vowel that does not change in quality during a syllable.

qualifier: a word or phrase that limits the meaning of, or attributes a quality to, another element, as in *black shoe*.

quality: the distinctive resonance, or timbre, of a sound.

quantifier: a word or phrase such as *plenty* or *a lot*, which allows you to refer to the quantity of something without being absolutely precise. It is often followed by *of*, as in *plenty of time*. Other examples of quantifiers are *any*, *both*, *each*, *either*, *neither*, *none* and *some*. Note that these words are not always used as quantifiers.

quantity: the relative duration of contrastive sounds and syllables.

quasi~: a prefix derived from Latin and meaning either *slightly* or *similar to, but not really the same*, as in *quasi-academic*, *quasi-literate*, *quasi-numerate*, *quasi-scientific*, *quasi-technical*.

question: a sentence so worded that it asks for information or a response.

question mark: refers to the punctuation mark (?) that is placed at the end of a question or interrogative sentence (as in *Who is that?*; *Where are you?*; *Why are you here?*; *When is your birthday?*; *What is the time?*).

question tag: refers to a phrase that is interrogative in form but is not really asking a question. It is added to a statement to seek agreement, etc. (as in *That was very loud, wasn't it*; *You will come, won't you?*; *He's not a friend of yours, is he?*; *She doesn't trust him, does she?*). Sentences containing question tags have question marks at the end.

quotation marks: *see* **inverted commas**.

quotes: *see* **inverted commas**.

re~: a common prefix in verbs, being attachable to almost any verb or its derivative, meaning *again*, *once more*, *afresh* or *anew*, as in *recount*. In most cases it is not followed by a hyphen; it should be, however, if its absence is likely to lead to confusion with another word (as in *recover / re-cover*). In cases where the second element of a word begins with *e*, *re* is traditionally followed by a hyphen, as in *re-enter*.

rebus: a device or puzzle in which a combination of letters, pictures and pictograms makes a word (especially a name) or sentence.

received pronunciation *or* **Received Standard:** the regionally neutral, universally clear, precisely articulated accent of British English.

reciprocal pronoun: used to convey the idea of reciprocity or a two-way relationship, as in *each other*; *one another*: *They don't appear to get on* *with each other these days; We try to help one another whenever we have the opportunity.*

reduction: in grammar, the lack of one or more of the normal constituents in a construction, as in *gone to town*; in phonology, a vowel that becomes central when a word is stressed; in historical linguistics, a narrowing of meaning.

reduplication: the process by which words are created by repetition, either exactly or with a slight change: *argy-bargy, hurly-burly, see-saw.*

reflexive pronoun: a pronoun which refers back to a noun or pronoun which has occurred earlier in the same sentence. The reflexive pronouns include *myself* (*I've hurt myself*), *ourselves* (*We did it ourselves*), *yourself* (*Can you do it yourself?*), *himself* (*He did it himself*), *herself* (*She has found herself a boyfriend*), *themselves* (*The children cooked for themselves when they went to camp*).

Reflexive pronouns are sometimes used for emphasis: *The judge himself ordered it.* They can also be used to indicate exclusivity, that something has been done by somebody by his or her own efforts without any help: *He made the arrangements himself,* and when *by* or *for* precedes a reflexive pronoun, it indicates that the person or thing that it refers to is alone: *I went shopping by myself; The brothers are cooking for themselves.*

reflexive verb: a transitive verb, the subject and object of which refer to the same person or thing, and which therefore takes a reflexive pronoun as its object, as in *He prides himself on his handwriting.* In many cases reflexive use is optional, as in *We enjoyed ourselves at the game* (reflexive) / *We enjoyed the game* (non-reflexive).

regionalism: *see* **dialect, localism.**

register: in phonetics, the compass of the human

voice, for example falsetto; as literary style, a
socially defined language form, e.g. legal English.

regular verb: *see* **irregular verb**.

relative clause: a subordinate clause which functions
as an adjective, often beginning with a relative
pronoun. There are two kinds of relative clauses,
the defining and the non-defining. A defining
relative clause is essential to the sentence,
because it defines the noun it is related to, as
in *Is that the woman who wants to buy your car?*,
where *Is that the woman?* makes no sense on its
own without the relative clause.

   A non-defining relative clause is not essential
to the sentence, because it only adds extra
information about the noun it is related to, as
in *I've just seen Mrs Smith, who wants to buy your
car*, where *I've just seen Mrs Smith* would make
sense on its own, without the relative clause;
see **defining relative clause**, **non-defining relative
clause** and **relative pronoun**.

relative pronoun: introduces relative clauses. The
relative pronouns are *who* (*There is the man who
drives the bus*), *whom* (*She is the person to whom I
sent the package*), *whose* (*This is the man whose
son I was at school with*), *which* (*They praised the
work which they had commissioned*), and *that*
(*That's the house that my teacher's moving into*).
Relative pronouns refer back to a noun, or noun
phrase, in the main clause. These nouns and
noun phrases are known as **antecedents**. The
antecedents in the example sentences above are
respectively; *man*, *person*, *man*, *work* and *house*.

   The relative clause may divide the parts of
the main clause; in *The teacher whose classroom
is closed is ill today*, the relative clause is *whose
classroom is closed*.

release: vocal organ movement away from a point of articulation, especially in making a **plosive**.

repertoire: the stock of languages or varieties that a speaker is able to use.

reported speech: *see* **indirect speech**.

resonance: synchronous vibrations in the vocal tract that are set in motion by phonation.

restricted language: a highly reduced linguistic system found in narrowly defined settings, such as weather reporting.

restrictive *or* **defining:** a relative clause that is an essential part of the identity of another element, usually without surrounding commas, as in *my sister who's ill*, *my mother who's all the family I have*.

restrictive relative clause: *see* **defining relative clause**.

retracted: the backwards movement of an articulator, such as the tip of the tongue.

retro~: a prefix derived from Latin and denoting action *back* or *in return* (*retrogressive*, *retrospect*).

retroflex: the sounds made when the tip of the tongue curls back in the direction of the hard palate.

retronym: a noun or phrase that has been adjusted because of a later invention, for example since the development of bonded leather and very convincing plastic simulations, *leather* may now referred to variously by the name of the animal (*calf leather*, *peccary*, *pigskin suède*) or *natural hide* but is invariably labelled as *real leather*.

rhetoric: the art of persuasive speaking, especially as practised in public oratory, and of literary expression. It can also refer to a high-flown declamatory style devoid of real content.

rhetorical question: a question which is asked for effect and assumes a preferred answer, or none at all: *What's the world coming to?*.

rhyme: an similarity of sound between words or
the endings of words, especially at the ends of
lines of poetry:

> *His beauty shall in these black lines be seen,*
> *And they shall live, and he in them still green.*

rhythm: the measured flow of words and phrases in
verse or prose, determined by the mix of short
and long (accented and unaccented) syllables.

riddle: a traditional utterence of a puzzling fact
or thing, intended to mystify or mislead.

root: *see* **base**.

rounding: the puckered appearance of the lips when
making a rounded (*u*) sound (*i* is unrounded).

runes: an ancient alphabet used in northern
Europe from about the third century, adapted
from the Roman and Greek forms for carving.

salience: the perceptual prominence of a sound.

scansion: the metrical scanning of verse.

second language: a non-native language that has
an official role in a country.

second person: a statement in the second person is
a statement about the person or people being
addressed. The pronoun acting as the subject of a
main or relative clause in the second person is *you*,
as in *You knew what was happening, so why didn't
you say anything?*. The pronoun for the second
person singular which is not acting as the subject
of a phrase is also *you*, as in *He told you that the
meeting started at six; We advised you immediately*.

The personal pronoun *you* does not alter its
form in the plural in English, unlike some other
languages. The possessive form of *you* is *yours*,
whether singular or plural, as in *He said to them,
'These books are not yours'; This pen must be
yours; I know that it is not mine*.

segment: a unit which can be clearly identified by its boundaries in the flow of speech.

semantic: relating to meaning in language.

semicolon: a form of punctuation (;). It is mainly used to separate clauses that are not joined by any form of conjunction, and where a comma would not be sufficient as the two clauses are grammatically independent. Although a full stop would be possible it would be too abrupt in such a case: *The children are tired; they are also hungry*. A dash is sometimes used instead of a semi-colon, but this more informal.

The semi-colon is also used to form subsets in a long list or series of names so that the list seems less complex: *The children were sent on a shopping expedition with a long list that included half-a-dozen eggs; 200 grammes of butter; 350 grammes of curd cheese; half a kilo of fat green bacon; a few tomatoes, and a couple of loaves of crusty bread*.

The semi-colon is also sometimes used before such expressions as *hence, however, nevertheless*: *Our friend Luigi who lives in Frascati was born in Kilmarnock; hence to us he will always be Jock*.

semi-vowel *or* **semi-consonant:** an intermediate sound that displays certain properties of both consonants and vowels, for example *w, y*.

sentence: crowns the hierarchy of grammar and so lies at the heart of the structure of language and literature. A sentence is a set of words, complete in itself as the expression of a thought, containing or implying a subject and predicate, and conveying a statement, question, exclamation or command. It may be recognised because it always begins with a capital letter and ends with a full stop or its equivalent, an exclamation mark or question mark. All the smaller grammatical units are

arranged within sentences; *see* **complex sentence**,
major sentence, **simple sentence**.
set phrase *see* **fixed phrase**.
sexism: the aspect of the English language that
has seen the most drastic change of recent times.
Traditionally in grammar, the masculine form
was assumed to include the feminine, by analogy
with the greater including the lesser; some
feminists took the view that this meant that such
vocabulary and grammatical features reflected
a male-orientated viewpoint, thus reinforcing
the low status of women in society and pressed
for change of both the expression and the status.

Vocabulary changes began by replacing 'male'
words with a generic meaning by neutral words:
salesman became *salesperson* or *sales assistant*.
Some uses of such terms, for example in job
descriptions, are now mandatory. Similarly *Ms*
is replacing both *Miss* and *Mrs*; *see* **letter-writing**.

In grammar, the lack of a gender-neutral third
person singular pronoun may cause problems, in
cases where nouns such as *pupil* or indefinite
pronouns such as *anybody* are used. For example,
*Each pupil who forgets [his / her] homework will
stay in at break*; for suggestions, *see also under* **he**.

Different solutions have been put forward to
avoid using the male pronoun in such a case, but
all have their critics. One alternative is to use
both male and female pronouns: *Each pupil who
forgets his or her homework…* , but it is very
clumsy, especially in spoken language. When
the subject pronouns are used, it is possible to
write *(s)he*. In informal speech, the pronouns
they, *their* and *theirs* are often used, but they are
not grammatically correct when a singular
pronoun should be used. The best way to avoid

all criticism is to reformulate the sentence using a plural noun, as in *All pupils who forget their homework will stay in at break.*

she: for a discussion of gender-specific pronouns *see* **he**.

sibilant: a hissing speech sound made by forming a groove across the tongue at the front part of the mouth, with the tip against the hard palate.

sigmatism: repetition of the *s*-sound for effect; also abnormal pronunciation of *s*, especially as a **lisp**; *see also* **alliteration.**

sign *or* **symbol:** a mark used in a writing system.

sign language: a system of manual communication that uses sign gestures, especially one used by the deaf, which in American English is *signing*.

simile: a figure of speech in which one element is compared with another of a different kind and said to be like it, as in *she's as bright as a button / brave as a lion / sleeps like a log*; *see also* **metaphor**.

simple sentence: a sentence with a single subject and predicate, and which cannot be broken down into shorter clauses, as in *The girl caught the bus*; *He watched her*; *They kicked the dog*; *see* **complex sentence, compound sentence**.

singular noun: refers to a single person or thing, *one* rather than *more than one*, which is the plural form; *see* **plural noun, irregular plural**.

slang: informal, non-standard vocabulary; the jargon of a special group.

sociolect: a linguistic variety defined on social grounds, such as a class or occupational group.

solecism: a mistake, or deviation, of grammar or idiom from what is considered to be linguistically correct; a blunder in the manner of speaking or writing.

solidus *or* **oblique:** a diagonal mark (/) which has various uses. Its principal use is to show alternatives (*he / she*; *Dear Sir / Madam*; *two / three-bedroom flat*). It may also mean *and* or *to*, as in *the budget for 1993 / 4*. It is used in some abbreviations such as *c / o Smith* (meaning *care of Smith*). The Latin *per* is sometimes shown by means of an oblique: *60km / h* means *60 kilometres per hour*.

some: may be a determiner, a pronoun, a quantifier or an adverb. It is used with *of* to refer to **plural** or **uncountable nouns**. It may be found in affirmative sentences, in questions when we expect an affirmative answer or when we want to encourage people to say *yes*. The word *any* is used in other questions and in negatives.

- Examples of the use of *some* as a determiner: *I'd like some bread, please*; *I'd like some olives, please*; *May I have some more rice, please?*; *Would you like some more wine?*.
- Examples of the use of *some* as a pronoun are: '*Wine?*' – '*Thanks, I've got some.*'; *May I have some more, please?*; *Would you like some more?*
- As a quantifier, *some* is followed by *of* and by a determiner or a pronoun, as in *I'd love to see some of your paintings*; *Could I taste some of this ice-cream?*; *Would you like some of these raspberries?*.
- As an adverb, *some* is used in front of numbers to indicate that they are approximate, as in *The headquarters is some 30 kilometers due west*.

sonorant: a voiced sound made with a relatively free passage of air.

sort: originally an individual letter, numeral, or punctuation mark as a piece in a fount of metal type; still in use for computer-set type, mainly for unusual characters called special sorts.

source language: a language from which a word or

text is taken, or has derived from; *see* **borrowing**.

speech: the oral medium of transmission of a language of a nation, region, or other group.

speech community: a group of people, whether identified regionally or socially, who share a common language.

spelling: the process of (correctly) naming or writing the sequence of letters that make up a word.

split infinitive: a phrase consisting of a **to-infinitive** that has been split by an adverb or other addition, as in *to gently push*. This was once thought to be a sin because it would have been impossible in Latin, the basis for English grammar. It is better to split an infinitive if this is clearer or less clumsy than the alternative: *I can't allow you to more than insinuate that he is dishonest* does not mean the same as *I can't allow you to insinuate more than that he is dishonest* and is clearer than *I can't allow you more than to insinuate that he is dishonest*. It may also be used for particular effect: *A sunny summer morning, perfect to not read* The Golden Bough.

spondee: a unit of rhythm in poetic metre, consisting of two stressed (long) syllables.

spoonerism: named for the Oxford University English scholar Rev William Spooner (1844–1930), this is the accidental or deliberate transposition of the initial letters or sounds of two or more words: *You have hissed my mystery lectures and tasted a whole worm*; *You were fighting a liar in the quad*; *You will leave Oxford immediately by the town drain*.

spread: sounds made with lips stretched sideways.

standardization: making a form or usage conform to the standard language.

statement: a sentence that asserts or reports information, as in *the house was burnt down*.

stative present: *see* **tense**.

stem: the root or main part of a word, to which affixes are attached.

stop: a consonant made by a complete closure in the vocal tract, a plosive consonant, such as *t*.

stress: emphasis on a syllable or word; syllables may be stressed or unstressed in various degrees.

stricture: an articulation in which the air stream is restricted to some degree.

strong verb: *see* **irregular verb**.

structure: a system of interconnecting linguistic elements, providing the language's framework.

structure word: s*ee* **function word**.

stylistics: the study of literary style.

subject: of a sentence or clause is usually either a noun, as in *Children cry*, in which *children* is the subject; a noun phrase, as in *The players in the team dislike him*, in which *the players in the team* is the subject; a pronoun, as in *He kicked the ball*, in which *he* is the subject; or a proper noun, as in *Paris is the capital of France*, in which *Paris* is the subject; *see also* **dummy subject**.

subjunctive: the mood of a verb which is least used in English. The present and past subjunctives are the same as the infinitive for each person (*I have, you have, he / she / it have, we have, you have, they have*) for all verbs except for the verb *to be*, which conjugates in the present as: *I be, you be, he / she / it be, we be, you be, they be*, and in the past subjunctive as: *I were, you were, he / she / it were, we were, you were, they were*. In the common expression *as it were*, the verb *were* is in the subjunctive.

    The subjunctive has three main uses:
- It can be used to talk formally about events which we imagine and would like, as in *If I were rich, I would sail around the world*.

The subjunctive is often used after *if*, *as if* and *I wish*, as in *I wish I were somewhere else*, but it is quite formal, and in casual speech or an informal style we would often use *was*, as in *I wish I was somewhere else*. There is one exception: we always use the subjunctive in the expression *If I were you*.

Sometimes *were* may be used with an infinitive, as in *If I were to tell you even half of what went on, you wouldn't believe me*.

• The subjunctive is also found after two types of construction:

(a) after the verbs *ask*, *command*, *demand*, *insist*, *order*, *recommend*, *request*, and *suggest*, followed by *that*, as in *The judge recommended that he not be released for at least five years*.

(b) after *It is desirable / essential / important / vital / etc that ...* , as in *It is vital that he be told before he leaves*.

These two types of structures are common in a formal style of American English.

• The subjunctive is also used in fixed expressions such as *God save the Queen*.

subordinate *or* **dependent clause:** a clause which adds to or completes the information given in the main clause. It cannot usually stand on its own as a sentence. Subordinate clauses are introduced by subordinating conjunctions, such as *after*, *although*, *because*, *before*, *how*, *if*, *since*, *that* and *when*. In the sentence *Although she was tired, she went to work*, the phrase *although she was tired* is a subordinate clause; in *I asked him how he was travelling*, the phrase *how he was travelling* is a subordinate clause; in *I didn't know that you'd decided to leave*, the phrase *that you'd decided to leave* is a subordinate clause.

Subordinate clauses can act as any element of the sentence except the verb; they may act as the subject, the object, the complement or an adverbial. This grammatical function can be tested in each case by replacing the clause with a single word:

- In the sentence *What he said is true*, the clause *what he said* can be replaced by the pronoun *it*. The sentence then becomes *It is true*, where *it* is clearly the subject. *What he said* is therefore a subordinate clause acting as the subject of the sentence.
- Similarly, in the sentence *I'll say what I think*, the clause *what I think* can be replaced by *something*. The sentence then becomes *I'll say something*, where *something* is clearly the object. *What I think* is therefore a subordinate clause acting as the object of the sentence.
- In the sentence *Chocolate is what you need*, the clause *what you need* can be replaced by *good*. The sentence then becomes *Chocolate is good*, where *good* is clearly the complement. *What you need* is therefore a subordinate clause acting as a complement.
- Finally, in the sentence *I saw him when I was in London*, the clause *when I was in London* can be replaced by *there*. The sentence becomes *I saw him there*, where *there* is clearly an adverbial. *When I was in London* is therefore a subordinate clause acting as an adverbial; *see* **adverbial subordinate clause**.

subordinating conjunction: a conjunction such as *although*, *because* or *when* which begins a subordinate clause. (Other examples of subordinating conjunctions are can be found in **subordinate clause**). Note that these words are not always used as subordinating conjunctions.

subscript *or* **inferior:** a small letter, numeral, or other symbol set beside or below the foot of a full-sized written character ($_r$); in contrast with **superscript** or superior, which is set beside or above the top of a full-sized character (^{r}).

substantive: a noun or noun-like item; expressing existence.

suffix: a letter or group of letters, for example ~*ly* or ~*ness*, which is added to the end of a word in order to form a different word, often of a different word class. For example, the suffix ~*ly* is added to the adjective *quick* to form the adverb *quickly*. A suffix is one kind of **affix**, the other being the **prefix**.

superlative adjectives: express the highest or a very high degree of a quality, and are formed in two different ways. One way is to add ~*est* at the end of the adjective, as in *cheapest*, and the other way is to put the adverb *most* before the adjective, as in *most curious*. The rules and exceptions are as follows:

- adjectives of one syllable form superlatives with ~*est* (*tall* becomes *tallest*), and adjectives ending in ~*e* add ~*st* (*late* becomes *latest*). Adjectives with one vowel followed by one consonant double the final consonant (*fat* becomes *fattest*). There are irregular superlatives: *bad*, *far* and *good* become *worst*, *farthest / furthest* and *best*. Also, *old* becomes *oldest* (regular superlative) or *eldest* (irregular superlative). The determiners *little* and *much / many* become *least* and *most*.
- adjectives of two syllables ending in ~*y* form their superlatives with ~*iest* (*happy* becomes *happiest*). With most two-syllable adjectives,

we use *most* (*tiring* becomes *most tiring*). With a few two-syllable adjectives, both kinds of comparative are possible, although the use of *most* is more common. These adjectives are *common*, *cruel*, *handsome*, *pleasant*, *polite*, *quiet*, *stupid*, *tired*, *wicked*, and words ending in ~*er*, ~*le* and ~*ow*. Examples are:
common: commonest / most common
cruel: cruellest / most cruel
gentle: gentlest / most gentle
handsome: handsomest / most handsome
hollow: hollowest / most hollow
pleasant: pleasantest / most pleasant.
- adjectives that have three or more syllables form their superlatives with *most* (*catastrophic* becomes *most catastrophic*). Words derived from one- or two-syllable words, like *unhappy*, that comes from *happy*, are an exception, and superlatives like *unhappiest* are used.
  Some adjectives by their very definitions do not normally have a superlative form, for example *unique*; *see* **adjective**.

superlative adverbs: are normally made with *most*, as in *The engine runs most quietly*. However, a few adverbs have a superlative form in ~*est*. The most important ones are *early*, *fast*, *hard*, *late*, *long*, *near*, *often*, *soon*, and in informal English, *loud*, *quick* and *slow* (these three adverbs are mainly adjectives; they are used as adverbs in informal English). There are also a few irregular forms of comparative adverbs: *badly*, *little* and *much* become *worst*, *least* and *most*; *see* **adverb**.

superscript *or* **superior:** a small letter, numeral, or other symbol set beside or above the head of a full-sized written character (ᶜ); contrasts with

subscript or inferior, which is set beside or above the top of a full-sized character ( ).

suppletion: the occurrence of an unrelated form to supply gaps in the conjugation of a verb, as in *go*, *goes*, *going*, *gone*, *went*.

syllabic: a consonant that can be used alone as a syllable.

syllable: an element of speech that acts as a unit of pronunciation, forming the whole or a part of a word and usually having one vowel sound, often with a consonant or consonants before or after it.

syllepsis: a figure of speech in which one single word is linked to a pair of words that are not related in any way, as in *He lost his hat and his temper*, in which the single verb *lost* is linked to both nouns *hat* and *temper*. The juxtaposition of these two nouns is rather unexpected, hence the effect; *compare with* **zeugma**.

synaesthesia *or* **synnesthesia:** a direct association between form and meaning (as in *water / wet*, *slug / slimy*).

syncope: the loss of sounds or letters from the middle of a word, as in *Gloster* for *Gloucester*.

synecdoche: a figure of speech in which the part is standing for the whole or vice versa: for example, *All hands on deck* where *hands* is used to represent sailors.

synonym: a word or phrase that has exactly the same or a similar meaning as another word, as in *mix* or *blend* for *mingle*.

syntagmatic: the linear relationship between elements in a word or construction.

syntax: the grammatical combination of words; the study of sentence structure, including word structure.

T

tag question: an element attached to the end of an utterance, as in ... *isn't it?*.

tap: a consonant made by a single rapid tongue contact against the roof of the mouth.

tautology: the expression of the same idea or fact twice over in different words, as in *one after the other in succession*. It should be avoided as it is considered to be a fault of style.

tele~: a prefix derived from Greek and meaning *distance*, as in *telecommunications*, *telepathy*, *telephone*, *telesales*, *telescope*, *teletext*.

telegrammatic *or* **telegraphic:** speech or written matter that omits function words and dependent content words, as in *dog chase cat*. Before the widespread use of telephones, urgent messages could be sent via the Post Office as telegrams for transmission by radio. They were charged at a rate per word, and so were as brief as possible.

tempo: the linguistic use of speed in speech, the use of a slow rate to express seriousness.

tense: the way a verb form changes to express when an event takes place, which is one of the verb's most important functions. For example, the forms of the present tense *to be* are:
I am, you are, he/she/it is, we are, you are, they are.
The forms of the past tense of *to be* are:
I was, you were, he/she/it was, we were, you were, they were.

These two tenses are used in many different ways to express moments in time: time that has past, the present time and time in the future, which do not necessarily have a direct link with the tense used. For example, in the sentence *I am leaving*, the tense of the conjugated form *am* is the present tense, but the sentence could be continued to mean that *I am leaving now* or refer to a future time, as in *I am leaving next week*.

The term 'tense' is often misused for reasons of practicality, and it is generally taken to refer to all the different forms of the verb phrase, i.e. *present perfect simple*, *future continuous*, etc; *see* **past perfect progressive, past perfect simple, past progressive, past simple, present perfect, present perfect progressive, present progressive, present simple, future, future continuous, future perfect progressive, future perfect simple, future time.**

tetrameter: a line of verse containing four metrical feet.

text: a body of spoken or written language with a definable communicative function, for example *news report*, *poem*.

the: the definite article, which usually refers back to something already mentioned, under discussion, implied or familiar, as in *What did you do with the car keys that I gave you?*; *Where is the dog?*. It is also used to denote someone or something as being unique, as in *the Queen*, *the Rhine*, and to denote a class or group, as in *the aristocracy*. *The* is sometimes pronounced *thee* when it is used for emphasis, to identify someone or something unique or important, as in *This is* the *book on the subject*; the *latest style*.

thematization *or* **topicalization:** moving an element to the beginning of a sentence to act as the theme, as in *Sunny today, isn't it?*.

theme: the element at the beginning of a sentece that expresses what is being talked about, as in *The key is in the door, it's jammed and won't budge*.

thesaurus: a book that lists words or phrases in groups of synonyms and related concepts.

they: *see* **he.**

third person: refers to the person or thing spoken

of, and not the speaker or the person or thing being spoken to. The third-person singular forms are *he* (*He should be here by now*); *she* (*She will get better*), and *it* (*It will be all right*) when they are the subject of a sentence or clause. The third person singular forms as object are *him* (*This would be a big bonus for him*); *her* (*He was unkind to her*), and *it* (*She did not like it*). The third person plural is *they* as the subject (*They are not here*), and *them* as the object (*He studied them carefully*).

Third-person singular possessive adjectives are *his* (*John rode his bike*); *her* (*June is worried about her mother*), and *its* (*The swan had broken its wing*). Third-person singular possessive pronouns are *his* (*Peter didn't bring a coat, but John has got his*), and *hers* (*Will you put this coat on June's peg? I think it's hers*). The third person plural possessive adjective is *their* (*This is their house*); the third person plural possessive pronoun is *theirs* (*They want this house to be theirs*).

The third person form is always used for formal invitations and for the replies to them: *Ms John Brown has much pleasure in accepting the kind invitation of Mr and Mrs Bloggs to the wedding of their daughter Josephine at 3.30pm on Friday 23 June at St Edmund's Church.*

though: may be used as a subordinating conjunction or an adverb. As a subordinating conjunction, it is very similar to *although*, but it should only be used in informal speech or writing. It introduces a subordinate clause which contrasts with the statement in the main clause, as in *Gaelic has been a dying language for many years, though children nowadays have to learn it at school*.

It can be used with *even* to give emphasis, as in

Even though I was very tired, I much enjoyed the party.
As an adverb, *though* has the same meaning as *however*; it is put at the end of the sentence, as in *Last night, I only watched TV. I had a good time, though.*

timbre: a sound's tonal quality, or *character*, which differentiates sounds of the same pitch and intensity.

to-infinitive: refers to the infinitive form of the verb when it is accompanied by *to*, as in *I was told to stay behind*, as distinct from the bare infinitive, without the *to*.

tone: the distinctive pitch, quality and strength level of a syllable.

topic *or* **given information:** the subject about which something is said.

toponymy: the study of the place-names of a region.

transcription: a method of writing speech sounds in a systematic and consistent way in order to produce a recorded copy.

transitive verb: a verb which takes a direct object. In the sentence *The neighbour's grandchildren broke the window*, *the window* is a direct object, and so *broke (to break)* is a transitive verb. In the sentence *She eats a lot of fruit in the summer*, the phrase *a lot of fruit* is a direct object, and so *to eat* is a transitive verb. In the sentence *You are meant to know how to solve this problem!*, the phrase *how to solve this problem* is a direct object, and so *to know* is a transitive verb. Common transitive verbs are *to bring, to carry, to desire, to find, to get, to keep, to like, to make, to need, to use.*

Some transitive verbs have an indirect object as well as having a direct object, as in *Don't tell me that!*, where *that* is the direct object and *me* is the indirect object. Some transitive verbs can

U

have a direct object, or an indirect object, or both.

Some verbs can be either transitive or intransitive depending on the context, such as *draw*, which is transitive in *I'm drawing the most beautiful landscape*, and intransitive in *I can't draw*; *see* **object**.

trigraph: a group of three written symbols representing one speech sound, as in *manoeuvre* (*man* [oeu] *vre*).

trill: a consonant, for example *r*, made by a vibration of the tongue; more common in an exaggerated form when sung, or in French.

trimeter: a line of verse containing three units of measure.

trisyllabic: a word or metric foot having three syllables, as in *relative* (re-la-tive).

trochee: a unit of rhythm in poetic metre, consisting of one long (stressed) syllable followed by one short (unstressed) syllable.

typography: the study of the style and appearance of the printed page, and the detailed knowledge of letterforms produced by mechanical means.

ultra~: a prefix derived from Latin and meaning *beyond* or *on the other side of*, as in *ultrasonic*.

umlaut: *see* **accent**.

un~: a prefix added to verbs, and sometimes nouns, to form verbs denoting either *not*, as in *untrue*, or it can also mean *back* or *cancellation of an action*, as in *undo*.

uncial: a form of writing consisting of large rounded letters typical of manuscripts of the fourth to eighth centuries.

uncountable noun *or* **mass noun:** a noun that cannot form a plural or be used with the indefinite

article. Such a noun is usually preceded by
some, rather than *a*. Uncountable nouns often
refer to commodities, processes, qualities,
states or substances, for example *happiness*. In
some situations it is possible to have a countable
version of what is usually an uncountable noun.
Thus *sugar* is usually considered to be an
uncountable noun but it can be used in a
countable form in contexts such as *I take two
sugars in my coffee please*. Some nouns exist in an
both uncountable and countable forms. Examples
include *cake*: *Have some cake* (uncountable) and
She ate three cakes (countable); or *light*: *She could
not paint for lack of light* (uncountable) and *the
lights went out* (countable).

uni~: a prefix derived from Latin and meaning
one, as in *unicorn*, *unicycle*, *uniform*, *unitard*.

utterance: a physically identifiable uninterrupted
chain of speech, lacking any grammatical
definition.

uvular: a consonant that is sounded by the back of
the tongue against the uvula.

variant: a linguistic form that is one of a set of
different forms in a given context, whether of
pronunciation, interpretation or spelling.

velar: a consonant that is pronounced with the
back of the tongue against the soft palate.

velaric: sounds, for example clicks, made when the
air in the vocal tract has been set in motion by a
closure of the soft palate.

verb: a 'doing' word, used to indicate an action,
state or occurrence, and forming the main part
of the **predicate** of a sentence. The verb is the
word in a sentence that is most concerned with
the action and is usually essential to the

structure of the sentence. Verbs **inflect** to indicate tense, voice, mood, number and person. Most of the information on verbs has been placed under related entries; *see* **activevoice, auxiliary verb, finite verb, ~ing, intransitive verb, irregular verb, linking verb, modal verb, mood, non-finite verb, passivevoice, phrasal verb, transitive verb, voice**.

verbal play *or* **speech play:** the playful manipulation of the elements of language, for example in **puns**, and the use of literary devices such as **paradox** and **zeugma**.

verb phrase: a group of verb forms which has the same function as a single verb, as in *has been seen doing*.

vernacular: the indigenous language or dialect of a particular country.

virgule: a slanting line used to mark a division of words or lines; *see* **solidus**.

vocabulary *or* **lexicon:** the set of lexical items (words) used in a language, or a particular book or specialism such as a branch of science.

vocal folds *or* **vocal cords:** two muscular folds in the larynx, near the opening of the glottis, that vibrate as a source of sound.

vocalic: pertaining to a vowel.

vocalization: any sound or utterance produced by the vocal organs.

vocal organs: the parts of the body involved in the production of speech sounds.

vocal tract: the whole of the air passage above the larynx.

vocative case: in English the case of nouns, pronouns and adjectives used in addressing or invoking a person or thing, as in *Peter, could I see you when you're finished?*, or some form of greeting, endearment or exclamation. It has more relevance to languages such as Latin which are based on cases and inflections.

voice: a form or set of forms of a verb showing the relation of the subject to the action. It is divided into active voice and passive voice; *see* **active voice**, **passive voice**.

voiceless: any sounds uttered without vocal fold vibration.

vowel: in speech, a sound made with vibration of the vocal cords but without audible friction, which can function as the centre of a syllable.

~ways: a suffix forming adjectives and adverbs and meaning *in the direction* or *in the manner of*, as in *lengthways, sideways*; *see also* **~wise**.

weak form: the unstressed form of a word in connected speech.

weak verb: *see* **regular verb**.

whisper: to speak very softly without vocal fold vibration.

who and **whom:** *see* **relative pronouns**.

who's and **whose:** are apt to be confused because they sound the same. However, they are not at all the same. *Who's* is a contraction of *who is* and is used in speech and informal written contexts: *He's the window cleaner who's afraid of heights*. *Whose* is a possessive adjective or a possessive pronoun indicating which person something belongs to: *That's the woman whose house you like* (possessive adjective); *Whose are they?* (possessive pronoun).

~wise: a suffix with several meanings. It can indicate *a manner* or *way*, as in *crabwise*. It can mean *in the position* or *direction of*, as in *clockwise*. It can also mean *with respect to*, as in

Y

familywise. It can also mean *clever*, *sensible*, as in *streetwise*.

word: the smallest unit of grammar that can stand alone as a complete utterance, usually shown with a space on either side of it when written or printed language, and potentially by pauses in speech.

word class *or* **part of speech:** a set of words of the same, or similar, formal properties or functions, especially their inflections and distribution, for example nouns, verbs, and so on.

~yse: commonly used in American English, but this is not a suffix. In words such as *analyse* and *catalyse* it is part of the original Greek, not a suffix.

Z

zero plural: a plural form that has the same form as the singular. It is the plural form of invariable nouns; examples include *cod*, *deer*, *sheep*. Some nouns have ordinary plurals and zero plurals as alternatives, for example *fish / fishes*. Nouns of measurement often have zero plurals, as in *Two dozen eggs please*.

zeugma: a figure of speech in which a single verb or adjective is linked to a pair of nouns, but one of the pair fails to make sense with the single word. An example is *Kill the boys and the luggage!*, where the word *kill* is linked to both *boys* and *luggage*. The association between *kill* and *boys* makes sense, but that between *kill* and *luggage* doesn't; the verb *destroy* would have made sense. Compare zeugma with **syllepsis**; the latter is often mistaken for the former.

HOMOPHONES

List of abbreviations

adj	adjective
adv	adverb
conj	conjunction
inf	informal
interj	interjection
num	number
ord	ordinal
pl	plural
pp	past participle
prep	preposition
pron	pronoun
pt	past tense
sl	slang
v	verb
vi	intransitive verb
vt	transitive verb

ail *vi* to be ill. **ale**.

air *n* the atmosphere; a light breeze; a tune. **heir**.

ale *n* a fermented malt liquor; beer. **ail**.

are plural and second person singular of the present tense of the *v* TO BE. **R**.

ascent *n* rise; upward slope. **assent**.

assent *n* consent; *vi* to agree. **ascent**.

ate *pt* of the irregular *v* TO EAT: *vt* to chew and swallow, as food; to wear away; to corrode. **eight**.

aural related to the sense of hearing. **oral**.

B *n* second letter of English alphabet; music: seventh note in the scale of C major. **be**, **bee**.

bail *vt* to liberate from custody on security for reappearance; to free (a boat) from water; to scoop out (water from a boat); *n* security given for release; the small bar placed on the stumps in cricket. **bale**.

bale *n* a bundle or package of goods or hay; *vt* to free a boat from water; (*with* **out**) to escape from aircraft by parachute. **bail**.

bard poet (old-fashioned or literary word) **barred**.

bare *adj* uncovered; empty; worn; *vt* to make naked; to reveal. **bear**.

barred *pp* of TO BAR: *vt* prohibit; secure; *adj* secure. **bard**.

base *adj* low; worthless; *n* foundation; support; a substance which reacts with acids to form salts and water; *vt* to place on a basis; to found. **bass**.

bass *n* the lowest part in musical harmony; the lowest male voice. **base**.

be *vi* to exist; to remain. **B**.

bean *n* a name of several kinds of pulse or peas. **been**.

bear *vt* to carry; to suffer; to bring forth; to permit; *vi* to suffer; to produce. **bare**.

bee *n* (*in full* **honey bee**) a stinging insect of the family *Apis* which collects pollen and honey and produces honey and wax and lives in large communities, often the domesticated *Apis mellifera*. **B**.

been *pp* of TO BE. **bean**.

blew *pt* of irregular *v* TO BLOW: *vi* to make a current of air; to pant; to cause to fly apart or be removed by an explosion. **blue**.

blue *adj* of the colour of the sky; sad; *n* the colour of the sky. **blew**.

board *n* a strip of timber, usually long and narrow; a table; a thin slab of wood or similar usually with covering used for some purpose, *eg* a chessboard; food supplied regularly for payment; persons seated round a table; a council; a group of people in charge of a company; the deck of a ship; *vt* to cover with boards; to supply with food; to enter a train, bus, ship, etc. **bored**.

bored *adj* impatient, tired; *pp* of TO BORE: *vt* to make a hole in; to pester; to weary by being dull, uninteresting or repetitious. **board**.

born *pp* of TO BEAR, to bring forth. **borne**.

borne *pp* of TO BEAR, to carry. **born**.

bough *n* a branch of a tree. **bow**.

bow *vt* to bend; *vi* to make a reverence; *n* a bending of the head or body as an act of respect or greeting; the curved forepart of a ship; *n* a weapon to shoot arrows; a rainbow; a stick for playing on violin strings; a slipknot. **bough**.

brake *n* a device on a wheel to reduce speed or to stop motion; a type of wagon. **break**.

breach *n* the act of breaking; quarrel; *vt* to make a gap in. **breech**.

bread *n* baked dough made from flour, usually leavened with yeast and moistened; (also daily bread) income; (*sl*) money; *vt* cover with breadcrumbs for cooking. **bred**.

break *vt* to sever by fracture; to rend; to tame; to interrupt; to dissolve any union; to tell with discretion; *vi* to come to pieces; to burst forth; *n* an opening; a breach; a pause. **brake**.

bred *pp* and *pt* of TO BREED: *vt*, *vi* to bring forth; to educate; to rear. **bread**.

breech *n* the hinder part (often of a gun); (*pl* breeches) garment for men worn on the lower parts of the body. **breach**.

brews third person singular of TO BREW: *vt* to prepare from malt; to concoct; to scheme; *vi* to make beer; to infuse tea. **bruise**.

bridal *n* a wedding;

adj belonging to a bride or a wedding. **bridle**.

bridle *n* the headgear used to control a horse; a restraint; *vt* to put a bridle on; to restrain; to express offence, resentment etc. **bridal**.

brows plural of BROW: *n* the ridge over the eye; the forehead; the edge of a cliff. **browse**.

browse *vt* to feed upon; to read through casually. **brows**.

bruise *vt* to crush; to injure and cause discolouration of the skin without drawing blood; *n* a skin discolouration from a blow. **brews**.

but *conj*, *prep*, *adv* yet, except, only. **butt**.

butt *n* the end of a thing; a mark to be shot at; an object of ridicule; a cask of wine; *vt* to strike with the head. **but**.

buy *vt* to purchase. **by**, **bye**.

by *prep*, *adv* used to denote the instrument, agent, or manner; at the rate of; not later than. **buy**.

bye *interj* shortening of goodbye; *n* in certain games, reaching the second round without playing an opponent in the first; a ball scoring a run in cricket without being hit by a batsman. **buy**.

C *n* third letter of English alphabet; music: first note in the scale of C major. **sea**, **see**.

cannon *n* a large gun mounted on a carriage; an impact and rebound; *vt* to collide with. **canon**.

canon *n* member of clergy,

staff at the cathedral; principle. **cannon**

canvas n a coarse cloth; sails of ships; a painting. **canvass**.

canvass vt to solicit the votes of in elections. **canvas**.

cast vt to throw; to throw off, to let fall; to condemn; to model; n a throw; a squint; a mould; a company of actors. **caste**.

caste n one of the social classes in a society. **cast**.

cede vt to give up. **seed**.

ceiling n the upper inside surface of a room. **sealing**.

cell n a small room; a cave; the microscopic unit of an organism consisting of cytoplasm and a membrane; a vessel containing electrodes and an electrolyte for current generation of electrolysis. **sell**.

cent n a coin worth one hundredth of a dollar. **sent**, **scent**.

cession n yielding up, ceding. **session**.

check vt, vi to stop; to curb; to chide; to control; n position in chess; a control. **cheque**.

cheque n an order, to one's bank, for money to be paid to the payee. **check**.

chews third person singular of present tense of TO CHEW: vt to masticate. **choose**.

choose vt to prefer; to select. **chews**.

chord n three or more musical notes played together. **cord**.

cite vt to summon; to quote. **sight**, **site**.

clause n a part of a sentence; a single item in a greater document. **claws**.

claws plural of CLAW: n a hooked nail; a crab's pincer. **clause**.

coarse adj rude; gross; crude. **course**.

cord n a thin rope; a band. **chord**.

course n a route; line of conduct; a track; a series of lectures; range of subjects; a layer of stones in masonry; a stage in a meal, eg dessert. **coarse**.

creak vi to make a grating sound; n a sharp, grating sound. **creek**.

creek n a small natural bay. **creak**.

cue n the last words of an actor's speech as a sign to a following actor; catchword; hint; the straight rod used in billiards. **Q**, **queue**.

curb vt to control; to check; n a check; part of a horse's bridle. **kerb**.

currant n small dried black grapes; the bush producing currants. **current**.

current adj running; circulating; n a running; a stream; progressive motion of water or electricity. **currant**.

cymbal n a musical instrument of two brass plates which are clashed together. **symbol**.

dear adj costly; valuable; beloved. **deer**.

deer n (pl deer) any hoofed grazing animal of the family *Cervidae*, the males of which usu have deciduous antlers. **dear**.

dependant n one who depends on another; a retainer. **dependent**.

dependent *adj* relying on; contingent. **dependant**.

dew *n* atmospheric vapour deposited on cool surfaces at night. **due**.

die *vi* to cease to live; to expire; *n* (*pl* dice) a cube with sides marked 1, 2, 3, 4, 5, 6, used in games of chance; a stamp. **dye**.

discreet *adj* prudent. **discrete**.

discrete *adj* separate, distinct. **discreet**.

due *adj* owed; owing; proper; *adv* directly; *n* a fee; a right; a just title. **dew**.

dye *vt* to stain; to give a new colour to; *n* a colouring matter; tinge; hue. **die**.

earn *vt* to gain by labour; to deserve. **urn**.

eight *adj*, *n* a cardinal number and its symbol (8); the crew of an eight-oared rowing boat. **ate**.

eye *n* the organ of vision; mind; perception; a small hole; *vt* to regard closely. **I**.

eyelet *n* small hole in cloth of sail or tent flap. **islet**.

faint *vi* to become feeble; to swoon; *adj* dim; indistinct; weak; feeble; *n* a swoon. **feint**.

fair *adj* pleasing to the eye; just; (weather) favourable; moderately good or large; average; *adv* justly; *n* a regular market or gathering for sale of goods. **fare**.

fare *n* food; the price of a journey on a public transport. **fair**.

fate *n* destiny; necessity; death; doom; lot. **fête**, **fait**.

feat *n* an exploit; a notable act. **feet**.

feet *n* (*sing* foot) that upon which anything stands; the appendages at the ends of one's legs; measures of 12 inches; groups of syllables serving as units of metre in verse. **feat**.

feint *n* a pretence (of doing); a sham (attack) intended to deceive (an opponent). **faint**.

fête *n* a festival; *vt* to honour; to make much of. **fate**.

fir *n* tall evergreen tree with needle-like leaves. **fur**.

flair *n* natural ability; aptitude; stylishness. **flare**.

flare *n* a sudden flash; a bright light used as a signal or illumination; a widened part or shape; *vi* to burn with a sudden, bright, unsteady flame; to widen out gradually. **flair**.

flea *n* a small wingless jumping insect, of the order *Siphonaptera*, that feeds on animal blood. **flee**.

flee *vi* to run away; to disappear. **flea**.

flew *pt* of irregular *v* 'to flow': *vi* to move, as water; to issue; to glide smoothly; to hang loose; to circulate; to be plentiful. **flu**.

flu *n* influenza. **flew**.

foot *n* (*pl* feet) that upon which anything stands; the appendages at the ends of one's legs; a measure of 12 inches; a group of syllables serving as a unit of metre in verse; *vt* to pay (a bill). **feat**.

for *prep*, because of; as a result of; as the price of, or recompense of; to serve as; on behalf of; in place of; in favour of; to the extent of; throughout the space of; during; *conj* because. **four**.

forth *adv* forward; abroad. **fourth**.

foul *adj* dirty; filthy; stormy; impure; obscene; contrary to rules; *vt, vi* to defile; to dirty; to strike against; *n* unfair play. **fowl**.

four *num* number 4. **for**.

fourth *ord* in a series, the item counted as number 4. **forth**.

fowl *n* a bird; poultry. **foul**.

fur *n* the short soft hair of mammals; a coating. **fir**.

gait *n* a manner of walking. **gate**.

grate *n* a frame of metal bars for holding fuel in a fireplace; a grating; *vt* to grind into particles by scraping; to rub against (an object) or grind (the teeth) together with a harsh sound; to irritate. **great**.

grater *n* utensil for scraping. **greater**.

great *adj* large; eminent; noble; chief; intense; excellent; skilful. **grate**.

greater *adj* comparative of **great**. **grater**.

grocer *n* a merchant who deals in food and household supplies. **grosser**.

grosser *adj* comparative of GROSS: thick; coarse; obscene; shameful; whole. **grocer**.

guessed *pp* and *pt* of TO GUESS: *vt* to form an opinion, hypothesis, or estimate of something with little or no measurement, calculation or information; to judge correctly by doing this; to think or suppose. **guest**.

guest *n* a person entertained by another; any paying customer of a hotel or restaurant; a performer appearing by special invitation. **guessed**.

guise *n* an external appearance, aspect; an assumed appearance, pretence. **guys**.

guys plural of GUY: *n* a rope securing a tent; an effigy of Guy Fawkes; a man or boy. **guise**.

hair *n* a thread-like covering on the skin of mammals; a mass of hair growing on the human head. **hare**.

hall *n* a large public room; the entrance room of a house. **haul**.

hare *n* any of various mammals of the genus *Lepus* resembling a large rabbit, with tawny fur, long ears, a short tail and hind legs longer than fore. **hair**.

haul *vt* to pull; to drag; *n* a catch (of fish); the distance over which something is transported. **hall**.

heal *vt* to make sound or healthy; to cure. **heel**.

hear *vt, vi* to perceive by the ear; to listen; to conduct a legal hearing. **here**.

heard *pp* and *pt* of the irregular *v* TO HEAR. **herd**.

heel *n* the hind part of the foot; the part of a sock or shoe covering it; *vt* (marine) to list or tilt; (football) to strike with the heel. **heal**.

heir *n* one who inherits. **air**.

herd *n* a large number of animals, *esp* cattle, living and feeding together; *vt, vi* to assemble or move animals together. **heard**.

here *adv* in this place; now; on earth. **hear**.

hi *interj* greeting. **high**.

high *adj* elevated; lofty; strong; (of price) dear; sharp; (of food) not fresh; intoxicated; *adv* greatly; in, on, or to a high degree or rank; *n* a high level or place; a euphoric state induced by drugs or alcohol. **hi**.

higher *adj* comparative of HIGH. **hire**.

hire *vt* to engage for wages; to lease out; *n* wages; payment for the temporary use of something. **higher**.

hold *vt, vi* to have in one's grasp; to confine; to keep; to contain; to occupy; to support; to carry on, *eg* a meeting; to regard; to believe; *n* a grasp; possession; a dominance over; the lowermost inside part of a ship. **holed**.

hole *n* a hollow place; an aperture; a cavity; a den; a small dirty place; a difficult situation; a small bound hollow to receive a golf ball; a fairway plus tee in golf; *vt, vi* sports: to send the ball into a hole. **whole**.

holed *pp* and *pt* of *v* to **hole**. **hold**.

hour *n* a period of 3600 seconds; a special point in time; the distance covered in an hour; (*pl*) the customary period for work etc; ~**ly** *adj* occurring every hour. **our**.

I *n* ninth letter of English alphabet; *pron* the first person singular. **eye**.

idle *adj* doing nothing; lazy; out of work; *vt* to waste or spend time uselessly; *vi* (of an engine) to operate without transmitting power. **idol**.

idol *n* a manufactured image or anything worshipped. **idle**.

in *prep, adv* within; not out; during; being a member of; wearing. **inn**.

incite *vt* to urge on; to stir up. **insight**.

inn *n* a small hotel; a public house. **in**.

insight *n* discernment; penetration. **incite**.

ion *n* an atom with one or more missing or extra electrons. **iron**.

iron *n* a metallic element, occurring naturally as magnetite, haematite, etc; a tool, etc of this metal; a heavy implement with a heated flat undersurface for pressing cloth; (*pl*) shackles of iron; firm strength; power; any of certain golf clubs with angled metal heads; *adj* of iron; like iron, strong and firm; *vt, vi* to press with a hot iron. **ion**.

islet *n* a little island. **eyelet**.

J *n* tenth letter of English alphabet. **jay**.

jay *n* brownish-pink bird with blue and black wings. **J**.

kerb *n* stone edging to pavement. **curb**.

knew *pt* of **know**. **new**.

knight *n* a rank conferring title Sir; a chessman shaped like a horse's head. **night**.

knot *n* a lump in a thread, etc formed by a tightened loop or tangling; a fastening made by tying lengths of rope, etc; *vt, vi* (*pt* knotted) to make or form a knot (in); to entangle or become entangled. **not**.

know vt to be aware that; to be sure that; to understand; to be acquainted with; vi to have knowledge. **no**.

knows third person singular of present tense of v TO KNOW. **nose**.

lacks third person singular of present tense of v TO LACK: vt to want; to need; vi to be in want. **lax**.

lain pp of irregular v TO LIE: vi to stretch out or rest in a horizontal position; to be in a specified condition; to be situated; to exist. **lane**.

lane n a narrow road, path etc; a path or strip specifically designated for ships, aircraft, cars etc. **lain**.

lax adj loose; slack; vague; not strict. **lacks**.

leak n a hole which admits water or gas; confidential information made public deliberately or accidentally; vi to let water in or out; to disclose. **leek**.

leant pp and pt of v TO LEAN: vi to slope; to incline; to rest against; to rely on. **lent**.

leek n long, fibrous green vegetable. **leak**.

lent pp and pt of v TO LEND: vt to grant use of a thing temporarily; to provide money at interest. **leant**.

loan n lending; something lent, esp money; vt, vi to lend. **lone**.

lone adj solitary; single; isolated. **loan**.

made pp and pt of v TO MAKE: vt, vi to create; to construct; to produce; to cause to be; to perform; to force; to reach. **maid**.

maid n a young girl; a female servant. **made**.

mail n letters etc conveyed and delivered by the post office; a postal system. **male**.

main adj chief; leading; n strength; the greater part; the ocean. **mane**.

maize n a cereal grass, Zea Mays, yielding large grains on a cob. **maze**.

male n one of the individuals in a sexually reproducing species which produces the smaller gamete; a man or boy; adj of this sex. **mail**.

mane n the long hair on the neck of a horse, male lion etc. **main**.

maze n a labyrinth; a perplexity. **maize**.

meat n animal flesh as food; the essence of something. **meet**.

meet vt, vi to come face to face; to encounter; to satisfy (of criteria); to assemble; adj suitable. **meat**.

metal n any of a class of chemical elements which are ductile solids, and are good conductors of heat and electricity such as gold, iron, or copper. **mettle**.

mettle n spirit; courage. **metal**.

mews n yard or street surrounded with what used to be stables. **muse**.

might n power; strength. **mite**.

mind n the intellectual faculty; intellect; reason; understanding; inclination; opinion; memory; vt to heed; to pay attention to; to take care of; to care about; to object. **mined**.

mined pp of v TO MINE: obtain

mineral by digging; to place mines that will explode when touched. **mind**.

missed *pp* and *pt* of TO MISS: *vt* to fail to hit, find, meet, etc; to lose; to omit; to fail to take advantage of; to feel the loss of. **mist**.

mist *n* a mass of visible water vapour. **missed**.

mite *n* a very small arachnid of the order *Acarina*; a small object or person. **might**.

mode *n* way of acting, doing, existing; manner; fashion; (music) any of the scales used in composition; (statistics) the most frequent element of a set. **mowed**.

morning *n* the first part of the day. **mourning**.

mourning present participle of *v* TO MOURN: *vi* to sorrow; *vt* to grieve for. **morning**.

mowed *pp* and *pt* of *v* TO MOW: *vt*, *vi* to cut down; to cut grass. **mode**.

muscle *n* fibrous tissue that contracts and relaxes, producing body movement; strength; power. **mussel**.

muse *n* poetic inspiration; *vt*, *vi* to ponder; to meditate. **mews**.

mussel *n* any bivalve mollusc of the genus *Mytilus* living in sea water or of the genus *Margaritifer* or *Anodonta* living in fresh water and forming pearls. **muscle**.

new *adj* recent; novel; fresh; unused. **knew**.

night *n* the period from sunset to sunrise. **knight**.

no *adv* expressing negation; *n* a denial; a refusal; a negative vote or voter; *adj* none. **know**.

none *n*, *pron* not one; not any. **nun**.

nose *n* the part of the face above the mouth, used for breathing and smelling, having two nostrils; the sense of smell; *vt* to discover as by smell; *vi* to sniff for; to inch forwards; to pry. **knows**.

not *adv* expressing denial, refusal or negation. **knot**.

nun *n* a woman belonging to a religious order. **none**.

O *n* 13th letter of English alphabet. **owe**.

or *conj* denoting an alternative. **ore**.

oral *adj* spoken; of the mouth; taken by mouth; *n* a spoken examination. **aural**.

ore *n* rock from which metals and other minerals may be extracted. **or**.

our *adj*, *pron* pertaining or belonging to us. **hour**.

owe *vt* to be indebted to; to feel the need to do or give out of gratitude. **O**.

P *n* 14th letter of English alphabet. **pea**, **pee**.

paced *pp* and *pt* of *v* TO PACE: *vt* to walk up and down; to determine the pace in a race. **paste**.

packed *pp* and *pt* of *v* TO PACK: *vi* to form into a hard mass, to assemble. **pact**.

pact *n* a contract; an agreement. **packed**.

pair *n* two things of like kind; a couple; a man and his wife; *vi* to join in pairs. **pear**.

parse *vt* to tell the parts of speech and their relations in a sentence. **pass**.

pass *vi* to go past; to die; to elapse; to be enacted;

to succeed in an examin-
ation; to cross; to utter; *n* a
passport, etc. **parse**.

passed *pp* and *pt* of *v* TO PASS.
past.

past *adj* gone by; spent;
ended; *n* former time;
prep beyond; *adv* by. **passed**.

paste *n* a plastic mass of
varied materials. **paced**.

patience *n* endurance;
composure under trial;
a card game. **patients**.

patients *pl* of PATIENT:
n an invalid. **patience**.

pea *n* small green round
edible seed. **p**.

peace *n* quiet; calm; freedom
from war or disorder;
a treaty ending a war. **piece**.

pear *n* sweet juicy fruit. **pair**.

pee *n* abbreviation of pence.
p, **pea**.

peer *n* an equal; a nobleman;
vi to peep out; to look
closely or with difficulty.
pier.

piece *n* a portion; a distinct
part; a short composition
or writing; a coin. **peace**.

pier *n* stone column
supporting arch, etc;
a wharf or landing stage.
peer.

place *n* position; room;
passage in book; rank;
office; *vt* to put or set;
to locate. **plaice**.

plaice *n* flat sea fish. **place**.

plain *adj* level; evident;
unflavoured; *n* a tract of
level land. **plane**.

plane *adj* level; flat; *n* smooth
surface; joiner's smoothing
tool; an aeroplane;
vt to make smooth. **plain**.

plum *n* round juicy sweet
fruit. **plumb**.

plumb *n* a lead weight

attached to a line used to
determine the vertical;
adj true vertical;
adv vertically; *vt* to test
with a plumb line. **plum**.

poor *adj* having little money;
needy; unfortunate;
deficient; inferior;
disappointing; *n* those who
have little. **pore**, **pour**.

pore *n* a minute opening in
the skin; a small interstice;
vi to examine or study with
care. **poor**, **pour**.

pour *vi* to flow continuously;
to rain heavily; to serve
liquid refreshment. **poor**,
pore.

praise *vt* to express approval
of; to commend; to worship;
n commendation. **preys**.

pray *vi*, *vt* to beg or implore;
to ask reverently. **prey**.

prey *n* a victim; animal
killed for food by another;
vi to victimise. **pray**.

preys plural of PREY as a
noun; third person singular
of present tense of **prey** as a
verb. **praise**.

prince *n* the son of a king or
emperor; *adj* princely.
prints.

principal *n* head of a school,
firm, etc; chief in authority;
capital sum lent at interest;
adj first; chief; most
important. **principle**.

principle *n* cause or origin;
a general truth;
a fundamental law; a rule of
conduct; uprightness.
principal.

prints third person singular
of present tense of *v*
TO PRINT: *vt* to mark by
pressure; to stamp; to copy
by pressure; *vi* to publish;
n pl of PRINT, a mark made

by pressure; an engraving, etc; a newspaper; printed calico. **prince**.

Q *n* 17th letter of English alphabet. **cue**.

queue *n* a line of people, vehicles, etc awaiting entry, a turn etc. **cue**.

R *n* 18th letter of English alphabet. **are**.

rain *n* moisture falling in drops; *vi* to fall in drops. **reign**, **rein**.

raise *vt* to cause to rise; to lift upward; to excite; to stir up; to levy; to breed; to abandon (siege). **rays**, **raze**.

rap *n* a smart blow; a knock; *vi, vt* to strike smartly; *(inf)* talk, conversation. **wrap**.

rapped *pp* and *pt* of *v* TO RAP. **rapt**, **wrapped**.

rapt *adj* transported; enraptured. **rapped**, **wrapped**.

raw *adj* uncooked; in natural state; crude; unripe; cold and damp; sore. **roar**.

rays *pl* of RAY, in a line of light; a gleam of intelligence; a radius; a flatfish. **raise**, **raze**.

raze *vt* to blot out; to demolish. **raise**, **raise**.

read *pp* and *pt* (when pronounced as *red*) of *v* TO READ: *vt* to peruse; to utter aloud; to explain; *vi* to peruse; to study; to stand written or printed; to make sense; *adj* well-informed, well-read. **red**.

red *adj* blood-coloured; *n* a primary colour. **read**.

reign *vi* to be sovereign; to rule; to prevail; *n* royal authority; duration of kingship. **rain**, **rein**.

rein *n* the strap of a bridle; restraint; *vt* to govern by a bridle; *vi* to obey the reins. **rain**, **reign**.

residence *n* abode; dwelling. **residents**.

residents *pl* of *n* RESIDENT: people who live in house, area, town, country. **residence**.

right *adj* straight; just; correct; opposite of left; perpendicular; *adv* justly; very; to the right hand; *n* truth; justice; *vt, vi* to put right. **rite**, **write**.

ring *n* anything in the form of a circle; a gold, silver, etc, hoop for decorating fingers; a circular area for contests; a group with mutual interests; sound of bell; *vt* to encircle; to cause to sound; *vi* to sound. **wring**.

rite *n* a solemn religious act; form; ceremony. **right**, **write**.

road *n* a public highway for travellers, vehicles; a highway; a surfaced track for travelling. **rode**.

roar *vi* to cry with a loud voice; to bellow; *n* the full loud cry of large animal; a shout. **raw**.

rode *pp* of *v* TO RIDE. **road**.

rung *pp* of irregular *v* TO RING. **wrung**.

rye *n* a cereal plant, *Secale cereale*; its grain; a whiskey made from rye. **wry**.

sail *n* a canvas spread to catch the wind; a voyage in a sailing vessel; *vi, vt* to move by means of sails; to glide; to navigate. **sale**.

sale *n* act of selling; market; auction. **sail**.

saw *n* a cutting instrument with a toothed edge; *vt, vi* to cut with a saw; *pt* of *v* to **see**. **soar**, **sore**.

sawed *pp* and *pt* of *v* to **saw**. **soared**, **sword**.

scene *n* a stage; a distinct part of a play; a painted device on the stage; place of action; a view; display of emotion. **seen**.

scent *n* an odour left by an animal, by which it can be tracked, a perfume; sense of smell; *vt* to discern by smell. **cent**, **sent**.

sea *n* an expanse of salt water, ocean or part of it. **C**, **see**.

sealing present participle of *v* TO SEAL: *vt* to set a seal to; to confirm; to close. **ceiling**.

seas *pl* of *n* **sea**. **sees**, **seize**.

see *vt* to perceive by the eye; to notice; to understand; *vi* to have the power of sight; *interj* look! *n* diocese or sphere of a bishop. **C**, **sea**.

seed *n* a plants reproductive unit from which a new plant grows; descendant; *vt*, *vi* to sow; to produce seed. **cede**.

seen *pp* of *v* to **see**. **scene**.

sees third person singular of present tense of the *v* TO SEE. **seas**, **seize**.

seize *vt* take hold, control or advantage of. **seas**, **sees**.

sell *vt* to give for a price; to betray; *vi* to practise selling; to be sold. **cell**.

sent *pp* and *pt* of *v* TO SEND. **cent**, **scent**.

session *n* the meeting of a court; a series of such meetings; a period of study; a university year. **cession**.

side *n* the broad or long surface of a body; edge, border; slope (of hill); bias (of ball); *vi* to support;

espouse (a cause). **sighed**.

sighed *pp* or *pt* of *v* TO SIGH. **side**.

sight *n* the act or power of seeing; a view; visibility; *vt* to see. **cite**, **site**.

site *n* situation; a building plot; the scene of something. **cite**, **sight**.

size *n* magnitude; the dimensions or proportion of something; *vt* to arrange according to size. **sighs**.

so *adv* in this or that manner; to that degree; thus; very; *conj* provided that; therefore. **sow**.

soar *vi* to fly upwards; to tower. **saw**, **sore**.

soared *pp* or *pt* of *v* to **soar**. **sawed**, **sword**.

sole *n* the underside of the foot; the bottom of a shoe; any flatfish of the family *Soleidae*; *vt* to furnish with a sole; *adj* single; only; alone. **soul**.

some *adj* an indefinite number; considerable; more or less; *pron* an indefinite part, quantity, or number; certain individuals. **sum**.

son *n* a male child or descendant. **sun**.

sore *adj* painful; tender; *n* an ulcer, wound, etc. **saw**, **soar**.

soul *n* the spiritual element in man; conscience; essence; a person. **sole**.

sow *vt*, *vi* to scatter seed over; to spread abroad. **so**.

stair *n* a series of connected steps. **stare**.

stake *n* a sharpened piece of wood; a post; that which is pledged or wagered; hazard (at ~); *vt* to mark with stakes; to pledge; to wager. **steak**.

stare *vi* to look fixedly; *vt* to affect by staring; *n* a fixed look. **stair**.

steak *n* a slice of beef or fish for grilling or frying. **stake**.

steal *vt, vi* to gain secretly; to take from someone. **steel**.

steel *n* iron hardened by addition of carbon; a knife sharpener; sternness; *adj* made of steel; hard; *vt* to harden; to temper. **steal**.

step *vi* to walk; *n* a pace; a grade; a rise; footprint; rung of ladder; (*prefix*) related to by remarriage. **steppe**.

steppe *n* large area of grass without trees. **step**.

suite *n* a retinue; a set of furniture or rooms. **sweet**.

sum *n* the whole; aggregate; essence; substance; quantity of money; arithmetical problem; *vt* to add up; to review main facts. **some**.

sun *n* the star around which the earth and other planets orbit; its heat and light; sunny weather; *vt* to expose oneself to the sun's rays. **son**.

sweet *adj* agreeable to the taste; having taste of honey or sugar; fragrant; melodious; kind; *n* a dessert; *pl* confectionery. **suite**.

sword *n* a weapon with a long blade and a handle at one end. **sawed**, **soared**.

symbol *n* a sign; an emblem; a type; a figure. **cymbal**.

T *n* 20th letter of English alphabet. **tea**.

tail *n* a appendage at the back of an animal's body; reverse of a coin. **tale**.

tale *n* story. **tail**.

tea *n* an evergreen shrub, *Camellia sinensis*; its dried leaves; a drink made by infusing them in boiling water. **T**, **tee**.

teas plural of noun **tea**. **tease**.

tease *vt* to pull apart fibres of; to torment. **teas**.

tee a small wooden or plastic support for the ball in golf. **T**, **tea**.

throes *n pl* IN THE THROES OF, in the midst of. **throws**.

throne *n* a royal seat. **thrown**.

throws third person singular of present tense of *v* TO THROW: *vt, vi* to fling or cast; to propel; to twist or wind; to utter; a cast at dice, etc; a venture. **throes**.

thrown *pp* of *v* TO THROW. **throne**.

thyme *n* any small aromatic herb or shrub of the genus *Thymus, esp T.vulgaris*. **time**.

tide *n* time; season; the ebb and flow of sea. **tied**.

tied *pp* and *pt* of TO TIE: *vt* to fasten; to constrain. **tide**.

time *n* the measure of duration; a point of duration; occasion; season; epoch; present life; rhythm; *vt* to regulate or measure. **thyme**.

to *prep* denoting motion towards. **too**, **two**.

toe *n* one of the five digits of the foot. **tow**.

too *adv* over; as well; also. **to**, **two**.

tow *vt* to haul by a rope; *n* haulage; fibres of flax or hemp. **toe**.

two *adj, n* the number next above one. **to**, **too**.

urn *n* container of ashes of cremated person. **earn**.

vain *adj* empty; fruitless; conceited; in ~, to no purpose. **vein**.

vein *n* a blood vessel which returns blood to heart; sap tube or rib in leaves; a seam of ore; disposition; mood; streak. **vain**.

wail *vi* to lament; to cry aloud; *n* a moaning cry. **whale**.

waist *n* part of body from ribs to hips. **waste**.

wait *vi* to stay in expectation; to attend; to serve at table; *n* period of waiting. **weight**.

war *n* a fight between nations; enmity; a contest. **wore**.

waste *vt*, *vi* to ravage; to damage; to squander; to grow less; *adj* unused; devastated; *n* a wilderness; useless spending; decrease; refuse. **waist**.

way *n* a track, path, or road. distance traversed; direction; condition; method; course. **weigh**, **whey**.

we *pron* plural of I. **wee**.

weak *adj* feeble; frail; foolish; vacillating. **week**.

wear *vt* to have on, as clothes; to waste by rubbing; to exhibit; *vi* to last; to exhaust. **where**.

weather *n* the general atmospheric conditions at any particular time; *vt* to be affected by weather, as rocks; to bear up against (storms, etc). **whether**.

wee *adj* (Scots) small; *vi*, *sl* to urinate. **we**.

week *n* seven consecutive days. **weak**.

weigh *vi* to find heaviness of; to reflect on; to raise anchor; *vi* to have weight; to bear heavily. **way**, **whey**.

weight *n* heaviness; gravity; heavy mass; pressure. **wait**.

whale *n* any of the larger marine mammals of the order *Cetacea*. **wail**.

where *adv*, *conj* at or in what place. **wear**.

whether *pron* which of two; *conj*, *adv* which of two or more. **weather**.

whey *n* watery liquid that comes from sour milk. **way**, **weigh**.

which *pron* an interrogative pronoun; a relative *pron*, the neuter of who. **witch**.

whine *vi* utter plaintive cry; *n* a wail. **wine**.

whole *adj* hale and sound; *n* the total; all. **hole**.

wine *n* the fermented juice of grapes. **whine**.

witch *n* a woman who practices magic and is thought to have dealings with the devil. **which**.

wood *n* a collection of growing trees; timber. **would**.

wore *pt* of *v* to **wear**. **war**.

would modal *v*. **wood**.

wrap *vt* to fold or roll; to envelop; *n* a shawl or rug. **rap**.

wrapped *pp* and *pt* of *v* to **wrap**. **rapped**, **rapt**.

wring *vt* to twist and squeeze; to extort. **ring**.

write *vt*, *vi* to form by a pen, etc; to set down in words; to communicate by letter; to compose. **rite**, **right**.

wrung *pp* and *pt* of *v* to **wring**. **rung**.

wry *adj* contorted; twisted; ironic. **rye**.